10
MINUTE GUIDE TO

UPPING YOUR SAT* SCORES

by Lisa Bartl

alpha
books

A Division of Macmillan Publishing
A Simon & Schuster Macmillan Company
1633 Broadway, New York, NY 10019

International Standard Book Number: 0-02-860617-5

Library of Congress Catalog Card Number: 95-080512

97 96   10 9 8 7 6 5 4 3 2 1

Interpretation of the printing code: the rightmost number of the first series of numbers is the year of the book's printing; the rightmost number of the second series of numbers is the number of the book's printing. For example, a printing code of 96-1 shows that the first printing of the book occurred in 1996.

Printed in the United States of America

Publisher: Theresa Murtha

Managing Editor: Lisa Wolff

Series Editor: Bart Astor

Development Editor: Jennifer Perillo

Cover Designer: Lori Singer

Designer: Barbara Kordesh

Production Manager: Kelly D. Dobbs

Production Team Supervisor: Laurie Casey

Indexer: Charlotte Clapp

Production Team: Heather Butler, Angela Calvert, Tricia Flodder, Beth Rago, Jenny Shoemake, Christine Tyner, Karen Walsh

Contents

Introduction

You're approaching "test day." You've heard so much about "that test," the one that's supposed to hold the key to your entire future. Try to relax. There are a lot of myths out there about the SAT I: Reasoning Test, and in this book we will dispel most of them.

This guide will help you through this trying time of your life. It will turn your worrying energy into energy you can use to attack the test with gusto. A little performance anxiety can be a good sign; it means you care about what you are doing. If you can gain the courage to transform the anxiety you feel into the power to attack the test, you'll make it work in your favor.

What the SAT Doesn't Do

The SAT I doesn't measure your IQ. You are not born with the ability to do well on the SAT I. Your SAT I score helps colleges understand your readiness to do college-level work. Colleges are looking to bring students to their campus who can succeed. And colleges understand that success takes many forms.

Your SAT I score also doesn't make or break your future. While it's an important factor in college admission, colleges are not looking for "brainy" kids alone. They want to bring in a freshman class that is diverse and multitalented.

And, finally, the SAT I doesn't gauge other skills and personal traits that will influence whether or not you are admitted to a college. If you have a special talent that isn't necessarily academic, make sure the college knows it. And be persistent. Colleges want students who work hard.

10 Minutes a Day Makes Test Preparation Easy to Take

If you've been putting off preparing for the SAT I because you don't want to wade through the mountains of information on the subject, this is the book for you. In it you'll find the key points you need to know to do your best on the SAT I.

Conventions Used in This Book

Throughout the book you will find useful icons to point you in the right direction:

 Timesaver Tip icons offer ideas that cut corners and avoid confusion.

 Plain English icons appear to define new terms.

 Panic Button icons identify potential problem areas and how to solve them.

So, are you ready to take control of your future? If you're like me, you tend to procrastinate when you face difficult (and boring) tasks. The reason I wrote this book is to make it easier for you to get started.

The Author

Lisa Bartl has seven years of national educational administration experience and 12 years of communications experience. She worked for the College Board in New York City for seven years, in part as the associate director of the New SAT Development Project, and has published numerous articles on the SAT. She has also served as editor of the *New SAT Newsletter*, columnist for the *College Board News*, and associate editor of the College Scholarship Service's *CSS Bulletin*.

APPROACHING THE TEST

In this lesson you will learn the basics about the SAT I: Reasoning Test—including what the test measures, its basic structure, how it is scored, and how much time it takes.

MEET THE TEST

The SAT I: Reasoning Test is sponsored by the College Board and administered by the Educational Testing Service. It's a three-hour standardized test that measures your ability to reason—a skill you've developed both in and out of the classroom over the past 16 years or so. Colleges use your scores along with many other factors (such as the numbers and types of high school courses you've taken, your grades, and the extra-curricular activities you've participated in) to analyze how well you can be expected to do in college.

For more information and help in getting accepted to the college of your choice, refer to the *10 Minute Guide to Getting Into College* by Dr. O'Neal Turner.

THE PARTS OF THE TEST

The SAT I is composed of seven sections: three verbal, three math, and one extra section that can be either verbal or math. Each section is timed separately, and you will be told when to begin and when to end each section.

Verbal sections are composed of analogies, sentence completions, and critical reading passages. Math sections are composed of regular multiple-choice, quantitative comparisons, and "grid-ins." The grid-in type of question is relatively new for the SAT. Instead of choosing one of several options, you will be asked to come up with your own answer to the problem and fill in your response on the answer sheet.

Testing the Test. The SAT I includes a seventh section of either math or verbal questions that does not count toward your score. These questions are being tested for possible future use. No one can tell which section this is.

Do All Sections. Make sure you try equally hard on each of the seven sections, because if you try to guess which section is the one that doesn't count, you'll most likely guess wrong and suffer the consequences!

SCORING THE TEST

The SAT I is scored on a scale of 200 to 800, with separate scores for verbal and math. The average score is around 500. But this score does not depend solely on the number of questions you answer correctly. It is a scaled score that also takes into account how others fare on the test.

When you are considering which colleges to apply to, you should review what the average and range of SAT scores are for those who are accepted to each college.

SUMMARY

In this lesson you learned the basics about the SAT I: Reasoning Test, including what the test measures, its basic structure, how it is scored, and how much time it takes.

DOING BATTLE WITH THE TEST

In this lesson you will learn the general strategy for taking the SAT I and you will discover 10 ways to help you do your best.

True or False: I can't possibly learn all of this so quickly. True . . . and false.

True, you can't cram 16 years of learning into just a few weeks. No one can. The SAT I requires you to rely on the knowledge you've learned over the years.

But the statement is also false. In fact, there are some specific steps you can take to help you zero in on what is really important—understanding the kinds of questions on the SAT I and how to best approach each one.

Just keep in mind that short-term preparation won't improve your ability to study; over the course of your educational career you should have learned how to study effectively. So you'll want to limit your short-term preparation to only 20 hours or so.

THE GENERAL STRATEGY

The general strategy for taking the SAT I is pretty basic. Within each section:

- Answer all the easy questions.

- Mark the questions (in your test booklet, not on your answer sheet) that you think you can handle later.

- Cross out questions that you really don't think you'll be able to answer, no matter how many times you try.

- Work on the questions you think you can still answer.

- If you still have time, review the questions you thought were easy to make sure you didn't make any careless errors.

- If you still have time, go back once again and try to answer some of the questions you were sure you couldn't do.

 Don't Overcheck! Check your work as you move through the test to make sure you don't make mistakes. But don't keep checking instead of trying to answer more questions. Don't obsess.

SPECIFIC TIPS TO HELP YOU ON THE TEST

Here are specific tips to keep in mind as you take the SAT I:

- Read the directions—*thoroughly*. If you know the directions before test day, you won't have to waste valuable time reading them during the test. Get a free booklet entitled *Taking the SAT I: Reasoning Test* (published by The College Board) from your guidance counselor and study the directions. Use the time you save to answer questions.

- Don't tarry too long on any one question. You can always come back to it if there's time (if it's in the same section).

- Pace yourself; don't rush. If you go too fast, you will probably make careless mistakes, and you will lose even more time trying to correct them. The idea is to get the answer right the first time.

- Mark your answer sheet carefully, filling in the ovals neatly and completely. If you change your mind about an answer, make sure to erase the old response well. Make sure there are no stray marks on your answer sheet. A computer, not a human being, will score your answer sheet, and you don't want the computer to misinterpret your intentions.

- Don't be afraid to write on your test booklet. Mark it up all over if you want. Cross out any answers in your test book that you've eliminated. Mark questions you want to return to (*within* a section; you won't be allowed to go back to a section once you've left it). Write in information next to a diagram if that helps. Just be sure to transfer your answers to your answer sheet. The computer will not see your test booklet, and you won't get any credit for answers you have written there.

- Read all the choices before you choose the *best* response. If you mark more than one answer to a question, it will be scored as an omitted question, even if one of the answers you chose was the right one.

Stay in Sync. Keep checking the numbers on your answer sheet against the numbers of the questions in your test booklet, *especially* if you skip a question!

- As a rule, questions that are grouped together go from easy to hard (except for the critical reading questions, which ask you to jump around in the reading passage). So do the easy ones first, mark those you can probably answer if you have the time, and mark those that are impossible. After you finish the easy questions, go back to those that show promise. Then, finally, attack the impossible ones.

- Use common sense when checking your answers. Is your answer in the general ballpark of what seems reasonable? Or is it way out in left field?

- The diagrams in the math section are drawn to scale. If the question asks that you calculate an angle, for example, make sure the angle in the diagram looks about the same as the angle you calculated.

- Know how to complete the grid-ins (see Lesson 10). This is a relatively new type of question that you might not be familiar with.

- Guess wisely, not wildly. You'll gain one point if you answer a question right, but you will *lose* a fraction of a point if you get it wrong (except for the "grid-ins," where you won't lose any points if you get it wrong, as you'll learn in Lesson 10). Instead of guessing totally at random, rule out some choices that are clearly wrong, then guess among the remaining choices.

Expect Questions You Can't Answer. This is normal, so don't panic. If you don't have a clue about how to answer a question, just move on. Remember that you don't have to get every question right to score well. In fact, depending on the version of the test you are taking, you have to answer only about half the questions correctly to get an average score.

OMITTING QUESTIONS

There are many times when it is wise to skip a question rather than to work at it and waste a lot of precious time. Here's when you should skip the question:

- You're getting upset.

- You don't understand the question (the vocabulary or concept).

- You don't have the faintest idea of how to even get started.

SUMMARY

In this lesson you learned some general test-taking strategies and quick tips that will help you do well on the SAT I.

3

COMBATING TEST FEARS

In this lesson you will learn how to deal with test anxiety as you approach the SAT I.

True or False: My life will end if I don't get a good SAT I score.

Of course your life won't end. Nevertheless, at this stage of your life, getting a high SAT I score probably seems all-important.

Test anxiety is a real phenomenon and it's quite normal. When you feel anxious, you need to learn how to deal with it—not push it aside, pretend it isn't there, or hope that it will go away. Denying anxiety will put you in the uncomfortable position of having its ugly head rear up and bite you at the *very moment* you need it least. That's the way anxiety works— it's just the nature of the beast.

DEVELOP SELF-CONFIDENCE

The following tips will help you develop a sense of confidence and will keep your fears about the test under control.

TAKE CHARGE

When you're taking the test, be bold! Be critical! Be skeptical about everything you are reading. By taking an aggressive stance, you'll be giving your best effort at "critical thinking"—which is exactly what the SAT I is trying to measure.

As you read this book, you'll be pushed continually to regain this aggressive stance. I say "regain" because it is human nature to shrink before the face of a foe. You must continually resist feeling intimidated, even though that feeling is the most natural thing in the world.

Think of the test as an adversary—an adversary against which you must fight hard. Get mad at the test if that helps. Make a pact with yourself that when you walk in to take the test, you will simply *refuse* to let the test get the better of you—no matter how bad it gets. Grow bigger than the test. Master it, conquer it—don't let it conquer you. That confidence alone can help you emerge a victor.

Stay Focused. Focus on the test and only the test. Then focus on one question at a time. Dismiss every other thought that your mind keeps wandering to, including the next question. You should be so focused that when the time is up, you should feel that you don't know where it went.

Don't Be Self-Conscious! Continually shift the focus off yourself and onto the task at hand (the test). If you are self-preoccupied, you might not notice or use all of the resources available to you—such as hints contained within a reading passage. Avoid the downward spiral of self-focus, self-doubt, self-blame, and high anxiety.

FIRST DO THE EASY QUESTIONS

When you take the SAT I, first identify and answer the questions that are easiest for you. Then spend time working on the difficult questions that you find more taxing. In this way you'll gain a sense of mastery over the test. Remember, don't let the test get the better of you.

DON'T COMPETE

Dismiss any thoughts that you are competing against anyone else. When you are in the testing room, it is just you and the test—*period*. You will be pleasantly surprised to see how the ability to focus on the task at hand (whether it is this test, a piano recital, a dramatic reading—any performance) is absolutely essential to doing well in college, on the job, and in life in general.

SET A GOAL FOR YOURSELF

In a perfect world with unlimited time to take the SAT I, you wouldn't have to pace yourself. Unfortunately, the test is timed (three hours), and you have the opportunity to answer up to 138 questions if you are so inclined. But remember, you don't have to answer all the questions to do well on the test. So, how should you manage the test?

Set a goal for yourself—a score you can realistically expect to get when you take the SAT I. Use score results of prior tests or practice tests to help set the score you want to achieve. Remember, the SAT I score is not the be-all and end-all (see the Introduction for information about other factors in college admission).

Also, remember that very few students achieve perfect scores, so set a realistic goal. If you expect too much from yourself, you're going to feel anxious during the test and lose points as a result. Take a practice SAT I (see Lesson 12 for a discussion of how to do this) to determine how many questions of each type you can expect to answer on the actual test. Knowing how many questions you can comfortably answer will help take the edge off your anxiety when you enter the testing room.

SAT Scores and College Admission. There are many factors besides your SAT scores that affect whether you are admitted to college. Furthermore, there is at least one college for everyone, and no one college is perfect for everyone.

Be Reasonable

If you don't put pressure on yourself to be perfect, and if you decide instead that you want to aim for an average verbal score of about 500, for example, don't worry about answering every question on the test. If you are aiming for a verbal 500, generally you have to worry only about half of the questions!

Setting realistic goals will go a long way in helping you avoid panic. Be an optimist! You have a choice: to worry about what you're doing wrong, or to feel good about what you're doing right. You decide.

Specific Ways to Combat Test Fears

Here are more specific actions you can take to feel in control of the test-taking experience:

- Sit down and figure out a strategy for how you'll attack the incredible amount of information you have to study. Make sure you include a calendar for when (and what) you'll study. Often, just by planning your strategy, you'll feel better about yourself and you'll feel the project (studying for the SAT) is manageable.

- Visit the testing site before the day of the test and learn how to get into the building, where elevators are located, and so forth. Feelings of being lost or late, or of forgetting your No. 2 pencils, will set you up for nervousness, panic, and thoughts of inadequacy or low self-esteem at a time when you need all the confidence you can muster.

Choose Your Weapons. Have everything ready the night before. You'll need to take the following items: (1) acceptable identification (which includes a photograph or a written physical description of you, your name, and your signature); (2) your admission ticket; (3) two or more sharpened No. 2 (soft-lead) pencils; (4) a good eraser; and (5) a calculator (if you are used to using one; it is not required). Make sure the calculator has fresh batteries. (For more details about calculator use, see Lesson 11.)

Ask Your Guidance Counselor. If you have questions about which types of identification are acceptable, how to register for the SAT I, what to bring to the test center, or where your test site is, first ask your high school guidance counselor. If you still need help, you can call Educational Testing Service at (609) 771-7600. Customer service representatives are available to answer your questions from 8:30 A.M. to 9:30 P.M. EST Monday through Friday.

- Although it is tempting, don't cram the night before. It will wear you out and make you more anxious, when what you really need is to be relaxed.

- So, after you've studied well, put your preparation materials aside and do something fun the night before. (Don't party or stay up too late, of course!)

- Get a good night's sleep.

- Arrive at the test center early (between 8 and 8:15 A.M.).

 Be Confident! Don't let test day get you down. You'll do better!

SUMMARY

In this lesson you learned a few things about how to handle test anxiety. You learned to take charge of the task, set reasonable goals for yourself, and set up a schedule or calendar with study times and study goals.

4

THE VERBAL SECTION: ANALOGIES

In this lesson you will become familiar with the basic types of questions in the verbal section and learn about the "analogies" questions.

TYPES OF VERBAL QUESTIONS

The SAT I has three types of verbal questions:

1. analogies (19 questions)

2. sentence completions (19 questions)

3. critical reading questions (40 questions)

Verbal questions ask you to understand:

- what you read

- how the different parts of a sentence relate to each other

- how word pairs relate to each other

 Do Short Answers First. All questions are scored the same, so do all the analogies and sentence completions (which generally take less time) *within* each section first before tackling the reading passages. (Note: you will not be allowed to skip from section to section.)

ANALYZING THE ANALOGIES

Analogies measure your ability to:

- understand what words mean

- identify relationships between word pairs

- find a parallel relationship among the answer choices

An example of an analogy appears at the top of the next page. Give it a try.

Example 4.1

KANGAROO : MAMMAL ::

(A) frog : amphibian

(B) bear : fur

(C) giraffe : neck

(D) bird : pet

(E) fish : aquarium

Solution 4.1

Answer: A. The key to doing well on the analogies is to discover the *most precise* relationship between the two capitalized words *before* you look at the answer choices. Chances are good that there will be more than one answer that appears to be correct.

For example, in the question listed above, (A) is the correct answer choice because a *frog* is biologically classified as an *amphibian,* just as a *kangaroo* is biologically classified as a *mammal. Bear,* choice (B), is not a kind of *fur; giraffe,* choice (C), is not a kind of *neck;* and *fish,* choice (E), is not a kind of *aquarium.* While *bird,* choice (D), is a kind of *pet, pet* is not a biological term.

GENERAL APPROACH: CREATING ORIGINAL SENTENCES

Before you look at the answer choices in an analogy, try to think up your own sentence describing how the pair of words in capital letters relate to each other. Then plug in each pair of words in your test sentence, dismissing choices that don't work. Keep revising your test sentence until you find the correct answer. See how the SAT I measures your ability to reason?

In the example above, of course, the sentence we created was *"Kangaroo* is a kind of *mammal."* Both choice (A) and (D) fit in the sentence, but (A) is more correct since it is more precise.

Remember to consider all possibilities. You might discover as you work on the question that you need to narrow general statements of the relationship or, conversely, expand relationships you are coming up with that are too specific. Remember, too, that words can have more than one meaning, and pairs of words often have more than one valid relationship.

You can count on the fact that parts of speech between word pairs will be parallel. So if you can't tell how a word in capital letters is being used (for example, if the word can represent both a noun and a verb), try checking the answer for a clue to a new meaning you hadn't considered before. The words in capital letters will be used in the same way as the words in the answers are used.

 Think Relationships! Remember, you are looking for relationships between pairs of words, not individual word meanings that match.

Here are some more examples of analogies. Try them.

Example 4.2

DECIBEL : SOUND ::

(A) calorie : weight

(B) volt : electricity

(C) temperature : weather

(D) color : light

(E) area : distance

Solution 4.2

Answer: B. Sentence to use: *Decibel* is a measure of *sound*. Likewise, *volt* is a measure of *electricity*. The only other unit of measure mentioned, the *calorie*, measures heat, not *weight*.

If none of the pairs works in the sentence you made up, make up a new sentence. Since many words have more than one meaning, it's possible the sentence you used as your test doesn't work for any of the choices. If so, try new sentences until one guides you to the right answer.

Example 4.3

PHARMACIST : DRUGS ::

(A) psychiatrist : ideas

(B) mentor : drills

(C) mechanic : troubles

(D) chef : foods

(E) nurse : diseases

Solution 4.3

Answer: D. Sentence to use: *Pharmacist* prepares *drugs*.

Example 4.4

ASTUTE : STUPID ::

(A) redundant : idiotic

(B) agile : clumsy

(C) lonely : clownish

(D) trite : ignorant

(E) intelligent : smart

Solution 4.4

Answer: B. Sentence to use: *Astute* is the opposite of *stupid*. Similarly, *agile* is the opposite of *clumsy*.

Example 4.5

INTERRUPT : HECKLE ::

(A) disrupt : intrude

(B) tease : hector

(C) maintain : uphold

(D) condemn : implore

(E) speak : perform

Solution 4.5

Answer: B. Sometimes the analogy is trying to probe intensity of feeling. For example, *heckling* is forceful and unpleasant *interrupting*. *Hectoring* is forceful and unpleasant *teasing*.

Example 4.6

CARNIVORE : MEAT ::

(A) carnivore : vegetables

(B) herbivore : plants

(C) vegetarian : vitamins

(D) botanist : herbs

(E) pollination : plants

Solution 4.6

Answer: B. Sentence to use: A *carnivore* eats only *meat*. An *herbivore* eats only *plants*.

Example 4.7

DISCIPLINE : ORDER ::

(A) military : rank

(B) authority : follower

(C) parent : child

(D) teacher : student

(E) training : preparation

Solution 4.7

Answer: E. Sentence to use: *Discipline* brings about *order* rather than disorder. *Training* brings about *preparation* rather than lack of preparation.

Example 4.8

SENSATION : ANESTHETIC ::

(A) breath : lung

(B) drug : reaction

(C) satisfaction : disappointment

(D) poison : antidote

(E) observation : sight

Solution 4.8

Answer: D. Sentence to use: An *anesthetic* counteracts a *sensation.* An *antidote* counteracts a *poison.*

Many Words, Many Meanings. Keep in mind that many words have more than one meaning. If, after you've created your sentence, you do not find a parallel relationship among the answer choices, try a different meaning.

ANALOGY TIPS

When working on analogies, keep these tips in mind:

- Figure out the relationship between the two words, using a sentence you make up.

- Choose the pair of words that *best* fits the original short sentence you made up.

- Consider *all five* choices before you pick your answer. The first one you find that fits may not be the *best* fit.

- Consider that many words have different meanings, depending upon how they're used in a sentence. You're looking for a relationship between two words, not which words are closest in meaning.

SUMMARY

In this lesson you learned about the three kinds of verbal questions and the key to doing well on the analogies.

SENTENCE COMPLETIONS

In this lesson you will become familiar with and learn ways to attack sentence completions.

Sentence completions measure two things:

- your understanding of vocabulary

- your ability to perceive how different parts of a sentence relate to each other

There are two types of sentence completions that appear on the SAT I: one-blank and two-blank. Here is an example of a one-blank sentence completion:

Example 5.1

Through his _____ he managed to cheat his partners out of their earnings.

(A) inefficiency

(B) ineptness

(C) machinations

(D) regime

(E) dealings

Solution 5.1

Answer: C. You should ask, "Through *what* (noun) does one cheat?" You should be able to answer, "Through unfair play, conspiracy, evil planning, or the like." A look at the five possibilities reveals *machinations* as the only possible choice.

STEPS TOWARD COMPLETE SENTENCES

Here are some helpful hints that will help you do your best on the sentence completions:

- Try to answer the question first without looking at the choices.

- When you think you know what kind of word would fit, then look at the answer choices. Chances are the right answer will be very obvious.

- Sentence completions often test your vocabulary. If you don't know a word in the choices, it will be difficult to figure out its relationship to another word. So brush up on your vocabulary.

- You don't need to know the subject that the sentence completion is dealing with. You should be able to choose the correct answer based on the context of the sentence itself.

- Pay particular attention to certain key words such as *not, never, although, because, however, if, but,* and *since.* They indicate the relationship between words.

- When you've made your choice, reread the entire sentence inserting the word or words you've chosen.

- Don't pick the first answer that works—consider all the possibilities. A later choice could make more sense than the answer you've selected.

 Don't Go for Clichés. Clichés can appear deceivingly simple. Chances are there will be more than one answer choice that will appear to fit.

Here are some more examples of one-blank sentence completions:

Example 5.2

The film was completely devoid of plot or character development; it was merely a _____ of striking images.

(A) renouncement

(B) montage

(C) calumny

(D) carnage

(E) premonition

Solution 5.2

Answer: B. A montage is a collection of images.

Example 5.3

She delivered her speech with great _____, gesturing flamboyantly with her hands and smiling broadly from her opening remarks through her conclusion.

(A) candor

(B) consternation

(C) acerbity

(D) verve

(E) innuendo

Solution 5.3

Answer: D. *Verve* is a synonym for *spirit*.

Example 5.4

As a result of a(n) _____ with her landlord, she was evicted.

(A) contusion

(B) alternative

(C) conflagration

(D) altercation

(E) aggression

Solution 5.4

Answer: D. An *altercation* is a heated argument.

TWO-BLANK QUESTIONS

The second type of sentence completion has two blanks to fill in. The first step is to insert the first word of the word pair into the first blank space and check to see whether it fits the context. If it doesn't, of course, the choice is automatically eliminated, but much of the time it will fit. The second step is to determine whether the second word of the word pair is in harmony with the sentence as it stands with the first word inserted.

Example 5.5

Normally a(n) _____ of dependability, he had let his colleagues down; now he could not face their _____.

(A) pillar ... smirks

(B) besmircher ... titillation

(C) paragon ... wrath

(D) bastion ... adulation

(E) anathema ... debts

Solution 5.5

Answer: C. Despite being a *what* (noun) of dependability did he let his colleagues down so badly that he couldn't face them? *Paragon, bastion,* and *pillar*—all symbols of strength or virtue—would work; *besmircher* (one who dirties) and *anathema* (curse) would not. Using any of the three, now focus on the fact that he had "let them down." What do people show when they are severely disappointed? Certainly not *smirks* (crooked smiles) or *adulation* (praise). *Wrath,* however, is a perfect fit.

Example 5.6

Though the concert had been enjoyable, it was overly _____, and the three encores seemed _____.

(A) extensive ... garrulous

(B) protracted ... gratuitous

(C) inaudible ... superfluous

(D) sublime ... fortuitous

(E) contracted ... lengthy

Solution 5.6

Answer: B. The "though" sets up a contrast: the concert was enjoyable but it suffered from some defect. The concert was *protracted* (too long), and the encores were *gratuitous* (uncalled for).

Example 5.7

A good trial lawyer will argue only what is central to an issue, eliminating _____ information or anything else that might _____ the client.

(A) seminal ... amuse

(B) prodigious ... extol

(C) erratic ... enhance

(D) extraneous ... jeopardize

(E) reprehensible ... initiate

Solution 5.7

Answer: D. The first blank calls for a word indicating information that a trial lawyer would eliminate because it is not central to an issue. The only possible choice is *extraneous*. Likewise, a good lawyer would not mention anything that might *jeopardize* (endanger) a client.

Example 5.8

The _____ of the house, fresh lobster, was all gone, so we _____ ourselves with crab.

(A) suggestion ... resolved

(B) embarrassment ... consoled

(C) recommendation ... contented

(D) specialty ... pelted

(E) regret ... relieved

Solution 5.8

Answer: C. No restaurant would advertise an *embarrassment* of the house, but you may logically conclude that lobster was their *recommendation*.

SUMMARY

In this lesson you learned how to approach sentence completions.

6

CRITICAL READING PASSAGES

In this lesson you will learn what critical reading is all about, grasp some general strategies, and learn how to wade through the reading passages.

The reading passages on the SAT I vary in length from about 400 to 850 words. Sometimes you will encounter a pair of related passages that question you about a shared topic or theme the passages have in common.

Critical reading questions measure your ability to:

- read and think critically
- discover the underlying assumptions of an argument
- relate sections of a passage to other sections or the entire passage
- understand and assess arguments
- recognize inconsistency in an argument
- think for yourself

The material covered in the passages come from various fields and may be fiction or nonfiction. Sometimes the passages contain introductions or footnotes. All the information you need in order to answer the questions is contained in the passages themselves.

TYPES OF QUESTIONS

There are four types of questions asked about the passages:

1. vocabulary, in which you have to determine the meaning of a word based on how it is used in context

2. interpretation, in which you have to draw a conclusion about a word, phrase, or the passage as a whole

3. evaluation, in which you have to demonstrate your comprehension of the main assumptions and viewpoints in the passage

4. analysis, in which you have to show how one point leads to another

Here is an example of a critical reading passage and sample questions. Take your time working through it (you're not being timed yet).

The following passage is part of a speech given by President Franklin D. Roosevelt in 1934. In it, Roosevelt describes his administration's efforts to cope with the effects of the Great Depression.

In the consistent development of our previous efforts toward the saving and safeguarding of our national life, I have continued to recognize three related steps. The first is relief, because the primary concern of any government dominated by the humane ideals of democracy is the simple principle that in a land of resources no one should be permitted to starve. Relief was and continues to be our first consideration. It calls for large expenditures and will continue in modified form to do so for a long time to come. We may as well recognize that fact. Relief comes from the paralysis that arose as the after-effect of that unfortunate decade characterized by a mad chase for unearned riches, and an unwillingness of leaders in almost every walk of life to look beyond their own schemes and speculations.

In our administration of relief we followed two principles: first, that direct giving should, wherever possible, be supplemented by provision for useful and remunerative work and, second, that where families in their existing surroundings will in all human probability never find an opportunity for full self-maintenance, happiness, and enjoyment, we shall try to give them a new chance in new surroundings.

The second step was recovery, and it is sufficient for me to ask each and every one of you to compare the situation in agriculture and in industry today with what it was 15 months ago.

At the same time, we have recognized the necessity of reform and reconstruction—reform because much of our trouble today and in the past few years has been due to lack of understanding of the elementary principles of justice and fairness by those in whom leadership in business and finance was placed, reconstruction because the new conditions in our economy as well as old but neglected conditions had to be corrected.

Example 6.1

The main purpose of the three steps mentioned in this passage is to

(A) increase imports

(B) decrease imports

(C) raise farm subsidies

(D) increase national surplus

(E) none of these

Solution 6.1

Answer: E. The main purpose of the three steps is stated in the opening sentence: the saving and safeguarding of our national life.

Example 6.2

The top priority envisioned in this passage is

(A) justice

(B) economy

(C) efficiency

(D) honesty

(E) relief

Solution 6.2

Answer: E. The first paragraph states: "The first is relief, because the primary concern of any government dominated by the humane ideals of democracy is the simple principle that in a land of resources no one should be permitted to starve." Then it reiterates: "Relief was and continues to be our first consideration."

Example 6.3

According to this passage, reform is needed to bring change in enterprises such as

(A) plumbing and heating
(B) food and restaurant supplies
(C) real estate
(D) banks and stock markets
(E) farms and filling stations

Solution 6.3

Answer: D. The last paragraph begins: "At the same time, we have recognized the necessity of reform and reconstruction—reform because much of our trouble today and in the past few years has been due to lack of understanding of the elementary principles of justice and fairness by those in whom leadership in business and finance was placed. . . ."

Example 6.4

According to this passage, two of the economic sectors that had been hardest hit were

(A) shipping and mining
(B) sports and the media
(C) radio and television only
(D) agriculture and industry
(E) medicine and real estate

Solution 6.4

Answer: D. The third paragraph says: "The second step was recovery, and it is sufficient for me to ask each and every one of you to compare the situation in agriculture and in industry today with what it was 15 months ago."

GENERAL STRATEGIES

Critical reading questions test your ability to understand what you read. Here are a few overall strategies to help you get through these questions:

- If the passage seems pretty easy to you, read the entire passage first before you look at the questions.

- If the passage seems pretty tough, but you think you can handle it, read all the questions *before* you read the passage.

- If you can't understand the passage at all, skip it for the moment but be sure to return to it if you have time. Since all questions count the same, why spin your wheels on a toughie when you can skip to an easier passage?

- Answer as many questions as you can about each passage before you move to the next passage. If you try to return to a passage later, you'll waste valuable time rereading it.

- Before you skip to the next passage, go back to the difficult questions and give them another try.

- You can usually rule out some choices quickly, which will make it easier to choose the correct answer from the rest.

- Even if you've already chosen an answer, be certain to read the other choices to make sure there isn't a better answer.

- Review any questions you weren't sure of.

- You don't have to answer the questions in order, so if you spot an easy one you can answer that one first.

- For the most part, every word in the passage counts, and questions could deal with words you've skimmed over.

- Focus on the points the author makes—they will be the focus of the questions.

 Be Choosy! Pick the passages that interest you first.

DUAL READING PASSAGES

Sometimes, the reading passages section contains questions about two related passages. An answer may be found within either passage or in both. Most likely, the questions in dual passage sections ask you to relate the two passages. But you don't have to memorize everything from the two passages.

Here is an example of a dual reading passage and accompanying sample questions:

Passage A—"An Unwelcome Visitor," a legend of the Iroquois

When the frosts were unlocked from the hillsides there came into one of the villages of the red men a mild and quiet old man whom none of them had ever seen before. He stood beside the field where the young men played at their games, and when some of the fathers approached to bid him welcome to their village and wigwams they saw that his body was covered with sores, and they made excuses to turn aside that they might not meet him. When none went to him and called him brother, he turned to the village and walked slowly from door to door of the wigwams. The women saw him and as he approached their doors they covered their children's faces that they might not see his features, and wished in their hearts that he would not enter. When the little man read their thoughts, with saddened eyes and heavy steps he would turn away and seek another habitation, where he would again see that he was not welcome and turn his weary footsteps from the door. When he had visited all the wigwams in the village without finding a welcome in any, he went suddenly to the forest and they saw him no more . . .

Finally there remained but two more villages to visit and he feared that he should find none who would bid him enter their homes that they might minister to his wants. At last, however, as he approached a humble cabin his eyes brightened, for he read in the heart of the woman who saw him coming that she had taken pity on his forlorn condition and that her hospitality would overcome the dread his appearance caused. Said the woman:

"Thou art welcome, my brother, for thou art a stranger."

Then said the strange man: "Listen, my sister: Thou of all thy race hast had in thy heart pity and love for a suffering and friendless creature that have led thee to give him shelter in thy house. Know then, my sister, that thy name shall henceforth be great. Many wonders shall be taught thee, and thy sons will be made chiefs and thy daughters princesses. I am Quarara, and bear messages from the Great Spirit."

Then Quarara described to the woman a plant which she went forth into the forest and procured. She returned to the hut and prepared it as he bade her, and when it was administered to him he recovered from his sickness and the sores left him.

Quarara remained at the woman's wigwam many moons and brought upon himself all manner of fevers, plagues, and diseases, and for each one he described the medicine root or herb that would perform its cure . . .

Then said the strange man, Quarara, to her:

"Thou, Oh! Sister, knowest now what the Great Spirit would have thee teach his children freely. Thou has been patient and kind and thy heart is filled with gentleness. The sons that shall be born to thee shall be called Sagawahs, the healers, and thou and thy family shall be remembered throughout all generations."

Passage B—"The Boy and His Grandfather," a tale of the Hispanic Southwest

In the old days it was not unusual to find several generations living together in one home. Usually, everyone lived in peace and harmony, but this situation caused problems for one man whose household included, besides his wife and small son, his elderly father.

It so happened that the daughter-in-law took a dislike to the old man. He was always in the way, she said, and she insisted he be removed to a small room apart from the house.

Because the old man was out of sight, he was often neglected. Sometimes he even went hungry. They took poor care of him, and in winter the old man often suffered from the cold. One day the little grandson visited his grandfather.

"My little one," the grandfather said, "go and find a blanket and cover me. It is cold and I am freezing."

The small boy ran to the barn to look for a blanket, and there he found a rug.

"Father, please cut this rug in half," he asked his father.

"Why? What are you going to do with it?"

"I'm going to take it to my grandfather because he is cold."

"Well, take the entire rug," replied his father.

"No," his son answered, "I cannot take it all. I want you to cut it in half so I can save the other half for you when you are as old as my grandfather. Then I will have it for you so you will not be cold."

His son's response was enough to make the man realize how poorly he had treated his own father. The man then brought his father back into his home and ordered that a warm room be prepared. From that time on he took care of his father's needs and visited him frequently every day.

Example 6.5

What is it that keeps the villages from greeting the old man in Passage A?

(A) He is a stranger.

(B) He is old.

(C) He is covered with sores.

(D) They are unfriendly.

(E) They fear attack.

Solution 6.5

Answer: C. In the first paragraph, "they saw that his body was covered with sores, and they made excuses to turn aside that they might not meet him."

Example 6.6

The word "minister" (Passage A, line 22) is used to mean

(A) mind

(B) tend

(C) assemble

(D) preach

(E) negotiate

Solution 6.6

Answer: B. Take care of, or "tend."

Example 6.7

The words "many moons" (Passage A, lines 42–43) refers to

(A) people's faces

(B) the name of a place

(C) a measure of size

(D) a length of time

(E) a strange natural occurrence

Solution 6.7

Answer: D. Moons refers to the number of full moons, or a measure of time.

Example 6.8

The last paragraph of Passage A could be called a(n)

(A) repetition

(B) fantasy

(C) oath

(D) summary

(E) blessing

Solution 6.8

Answer: E. Quarara blesses the woman.

Example 6.9

One difference between Passage A and Passage B is that

(A) Passage A takes place in the past
(B) people in Passage B ignore an old man
(C) people in Passage A ignore an old man
(D) Passage A deals with illness as well as age
(E) Passage B has no moral

Solution 6.9

Answer: D. Both take place in the past; in both, people ignore an old man; and Passage B does have a moral.

Example 6.10

The woman in Passage A and the man in Passage B learn that

(A) illness is not a crime
(B) respecting one's elders can be beneficial
(C) children may understand more than adults
(D) both A and B
(E) both B and C

Solution 6.10

Answer: B. There is no mention of crime, and there are no children in Passage A. Since neither choice A nor C are correct, only choice B is correct.

Details, Details! Pay attention to the details in a passage—they are there for a reason.

WAYS TO GET THROUGH THE READING PASSAGES

Here are tips that can help you with the reading passages:

- Glance at the passage and, if you don't like it, find one you do like to start with. Read the passages that are interesting to you first, then do the others.

- Read the passage slowly and carefully, paying attention to details and key words. Try to understand the general meaning, tone, and key ideas.

- Don't spend a lot of time taking notes. But you can jot down your thoughts to help you answer the questions that follow.

- Read each question and the answers thoroughly and carefully. Sometimes one answer looks very similar to another. Don't choose the first answer that appears correct; a later choice may be a *better* answer. Make sure you answer the question that is being asked.

- Be thorough! Don't go on to another reading passage until you understand the passage and the questions completely.

Do the Vocabulary Questions First! Questions that ask about vocabulary in the context of a sentence take the shortest amount of time.

- Choose the *best* answer to each question. Some answers will be partially correct. Make sure your choice is completely correct.

Remember! Words have different meanings. Consider the context.

- When there are dual reading passages, think about the relationship between the two passages taken together. Ask yourself what they have in common.

- You don't have to know the subject being written about—all the answers will be contained in the passage(s).

Be Bookish! The best way to improve your performance on the reading passages is to read, read, and read some more.

SUMMARY

In this lesson you learned ways to approach the critical reading passages.

7

APPROACHING THE MATH SECTION

In this lesson you will learn which mathematical concepts you should know before taking the SAT I Math test, and you will become familiar with the basic types of questions asked.

The questions in the math section of the SAT I may ask you to perform calculations, manipulate equations, and figure out relationships. To solve many questions you will have to quantify words (literal expressions) or figure out a way to express them in an algebraic equation.

No Need to Memorize. Basic formulas are listed in the test booklet, so you don't need to memorize them.

Math to Review before the Test

Most math questions on the SAT I assume you've had a year of algebra and some geometry. You should be familiar with the following mathematical subjects.

Arithmetic

Here is a list of some general arithmetic concepts that you should know:

- basic addition, subtraction, multiplication, and division of integers and fractions
- percentages
- data interpretation (including mean, median, and mode)
- odd and even numbers
- prime numbers
- divisibility rules

Algebra

It will be helpful to know the following algebraic concepts:

- negative numbers
- substitution
- simplifying algebraic expressions
- simple factoring

- linear equations

- inequalities

- simple quadratic equations

- positive integer exponents

- roots of numbers

- sequences

GEOMETRY

While you won't be asked to give formal proofs of theorems in the test, you will need to use logic and knowledge of formulas. Make sure you know the principles involved with:

- areas

- perimeters

- triangles (including right triangles and the Pythagorean Theorem)

- coordinate geometry

- parallel and perpendicular lines

- polygons

- circles

- volumes

- slope

OTHER MATH CONCEPTS YOU SHOULD KNOW

- logical reasoning
- newly defined symbols
- probability

TYPES OF QUESTIONS

The SAT I has three types of math questions:

1. standard five-choice multiple-choice (35)

2. quantitative comparisons (15)

3. grid-ins (10) (called "Student-Produced Responses" on the SAT I)

In the math sections, the questions are grouped by question type. There are a total of 60 questions: 35 multiple-choice, 15 quantitative comparisons, and 10 student-produced responses.

Math concepts can be tested in any order. You might encounter algebra, geometry, arithmetic, then go back to geometry, and so on. So don't be surprised if you have to keep shifting your thinking gears; this is normal.

QUICK STRATEGIES FOR IMPROVING YOUR SCORE ON THE MATH SECTION

Here are some other strategies for improving your success with the math problems:

- Start with the questions you can answer quickly and easily. Then attack the longer, more difficult questions.

- Draw figures in your booklet (not on the answer sheet!) to help you visualize the answers to problems.

- Write measurements or values right on the diagrams provided in your test booklet.

- You are not expected to do computations in your head. Write out calculations on your booklet so you can check your work later. Just make sure to transfer your answers to the answer sheet. You won't receive any credit for the work you show in your booklet.

- If you feel like you are getting bogged down in calculations, you may have overlooked a shortcut.

- With more difficult questions, first try solving the problem on your own. Then look at the answer choices.

SUMMARY

In this lesson you learned which mathematical concepts you should know before taking the SAT I Math test, what types of math questions are asked on the test, and some strategies for improving your score.

8

TACKLING
MULTIPLE-CHOICE
MATH QUESTIONS

In this lesson you will become familiar with the standard SAT I multiple-choice math questions.

Standard multiple-choice questions test your knowledge of arithmetic, algebra, and geometry. You are asked to select the correct solution from five choices given.

Below is an example of a typical SAT I multiple-choice math question.

Example 8.1

If 20% of a number is 8, what is 25% of the number?

(A) 2

(B) 10

(C) 12

(D) 11

(E) 15

Solution 8.1

Answer: B.

$(.2)x = 8$

$x = {}^8/_{.2}$

$x = 40$

$.25 (40) = 10$

SOLVING MULTIPLE-CHOICE MATH QUESTIONS

Generally, you can use more than one approach to solve the SAT I multiple-choice math questions correctly. For instance:

- You simply know the answer and can deal with the question quickly, as in two plus two equals four.

- You can take the given facts and apply your knowledge to work out a solution.

- You may be able to back into the correct answer by eliminating answers one by one.

- You may be able to back into the correct answer by testing each answer until you find one that works.

Remember, there is a penalty for wrong answers. If the question is one you don't know the answer to, can't solve, or is too hard to use a process of elimination, you may be better off skipping it.

Expect New Symbols! On the SAT I Math section you will probably encounter at least one question that contains a newly defined symbol. All you have to do is understand the definition of the special symbol and pay attention to the instructions. The symbol is there to test your ability to reason with new information.

Example 8.2

Four "ABCD" equals three "EFGH." Four "EFGH" equals five "IJKL." How many "ABCD" are equal to fifteen "IJKL"?

(A) 4

(B) 8

(C) 12

(D) 16

(E) 20

Solution 8.2

Answer: D. Two ratios are given, and "EFGH" is the common link between them.

4 "ABCD"=3 "EFGH"

4 "EFGH"=5 "IJKL"

WHICH QUESTIONS TO ATTACK FIRST

Students use different approaches when taking tests, in particular when deciding which questions to answer first. Some students like the idea of attacking complicated, challenging questions first. They like the idea of rolling up their sleeves and getting "into" the question.

Other students like to skip the complicated questions that require "solutions" rather than "answers"; they would rather answer the straightforward questions first and then go back to the toughies.

 Easy Does It. Remember, the easiest math questions appear at the beginning of each section. Do those first.

While neither is the *right* way for test taking as a rule, the second approach is usually more appropriate for the SAT I Math test. The reason: all the questions count the same. If one problem takes you five minutes, and another only 20 seconds, you don't get extra credit for the time-consuming one.

 Timing Is Everything. The more involved questions generally appear at the end of each section. Be aware of how far along you are in each section and pace yourself accordingly.

BASIC PROBLEM-SOLVING TIPS

Increase your odds of getting the right answer by using the following steps:

1. Decide what the question is asking. Circle key words that tell you this.

2. Break down the question into manageable parts.

3. If you don't know what you need to know, ask yourself if there is a different way to approach the problem.

EXAMPLES OF MULTIPLE-CHOICE MATH QUESTIONS

Following are examples of SAT I Math questions with explanations of how they can be solved. Try to solve each one on your own first before looking at the solution provided.

Example 8.3

If $(x + y)^2 = 17$, and $xy = 3$, then $x^2 + y^2 =$

(A) 11

(B) 14

(C) 17

(D) 20

(E) 23

Solution 8.3

Answer: A. This is an example of a linear equation problem. In this question you are given two basic formulas containing two letters that have unknown qualities, and you are asked to find out the value of a third formula. To do so, you can manipulate the first equation using your basic understanding of how algebraic formulas can be restructured, and insert the second equation into the first.

$$x+y^2 = 17$$

$$(x+y)(x+y) = 17$$

$$x^2 + 2xy + y^2 = 17$$

Since $xy = 3$, then $2xy = 6$, and, plugging into that first formula,

$$x^2 + 6 + y^2 = 17$$

$$x^2 + y^2 = 11$$

Here's a quicker way to answer this question using estimates:
Since $(x+y)^2 = 17$,
Then $x+y$ must be just a little more than 4 ($4^2=16$)
Let's say that $x=2$, then y would equal about 2. In this case, $x^2=4$, so y^2=about 5, and $x^2+ y^2$=about 9. The closest answer among the answer choices is answer A: 11.

Example 8.4

If $x + 3$ is a multiple of 3, which of the following is *not* a multiple of 3?
   (A) x (B) $x + 6$ (C) $6x + 18$ (D) $2x + 6$ (E) $3x + 5$

Solution 8.4

Answer: E.

Solution: Multiples of 3 are 3 apart.

x is 3 less than $x + 3$.
$x + 6$ is 3 above $x + 3$.
$6x + 18 = 6(x + 3)$.
$2x + 6 = 2(x + 3)$.
$3x + 5$ does not have a factor of 3, nor is it a multiple of $x + 3$.

Example 8.5

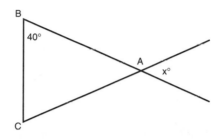

In the figure above, AB = AC. Then x =

(A) 40°   (B) 80°   (C) 100°   (D) 60°   (E) 90°

Solution 8.5

Answer: C

To do well on the SAT I you have to know some basic facts about geometry. In this case, you have to know that the angle you are trying to determine, Angle x, equals Angle BAC. Then, you also have to know that if the two sides are equal (AB = AC), then the two opposite angles are equal (Angle B = Angle C). And, finally, you have to know that the sum of the angles in a triangle is 180 degrees.

Since AB = AC, Angle C = Angle B, or 40°.
The sum of the angles in a triangle is 180°, so
Angle BAC = 180° - 80° = 100°.

Angle x = Angle BAC, so Angle x = 100°.

Example 8.6

The toll on the Islands Bridge is $1.00 for a car and driver and $.75 for each additional passenger. How many people were riding in a car for which the toll was $3.25?

(A) 2   (B) 3   (C) 4   (D) 5   (E) 6

Solution 8.6

Answer: C.

Solution: The basic toll is $1.00, so the extra toll is $2.25. $2.25 = 3($.75), so the car holds the driver plus 3 extra passengers, or 4 people.

Example 8.7

The figure below is composed of 5 equal squares. If the area of the figure is 125, find its perimeter.

  (A) 60   (B) 100   (C) 80   (D) 75   (E) 20

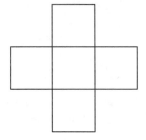

Solution 8.7

Answer: A.

This question involves a little bit of geometry and arithmetic. Remember, you are working against the clock, so you want to be able to find the quickest solution. Usually that means using your powers of reasoning.

The question states that there are 5 equal squares and the total area is 125. Therefore, the area of each little square is one-fifth of the total, or 25. The area of each square is one side times itself, or 5. The perimeter is made up of 12 sides so 12(5) = 60.

Another common solution to linear equations involves finding common coefficients and then isolating for the unknown. This type of question may use numbers or letters. Here's an example:

Example 8.8

Solve for x:

ax + by = c

dx + ey = f

(A) $\dfrac{ce+bf}{ae-db}$

(B) $\dfrac{ae-db}{ce-bf}$

(C) $\dfrac{ce-bf}{ae+db}$

(D) $\dfrac{ce-bf}{ae-db}$

(E) $\dfrac{ae+db}{ce+bf}$

Solution 8.8

Answer: D.

Multiply the first equation by e, so

axe + bye = ce

Multiply the second equation by b, so

dxb + eyb = bf

Now subtract the two equations (since the y coefficient is the same in each, you are canceling them out and eliminating the y):

$$\begin{array}{r} axe + bye = ce \\ -\ \ dxb + eyb = bf \\ \hline axe - dxb = ce - bf \end{array}$$

Factor out the x and you get x(ae - db) = ce - bf

and $x = \dfrac{ce - bf}{ae - db}$

Example 8.9

If $y = x^2$

$z = x^3$

and $w = xy$,

then $y^2 + 2^2 + w^2 =$

(A) $x^2 + x^6 + x^{10}$

(B) $x^4 + 2x^5$

(C) $x^4 + 2x^6$

(D) $2x^9$

(E) $2x^{10}$

Solution 8.9

Answer: C.

$w = xy = x(x^2) = x^3$

$y^2 + z^2 + w^2 = (x^2)^2 + (x^3)^2 + (x^3)^2$

$= x^4 + x^6 + x^6$

$= x^4 + 2x^6$

SUMMARY

In this lesson you became familiar with the basic types of questions on the math section and learned about the regular multiple-choice math questions.

QUANTITATIVE COMPARISONS

In this lesson you will learn about the quantitative comparison math questions.

Following is an example of the directions for the quantitative comparison questions. Refer to this when looking at the examples in this chapter.

<table>
<tr>
<td>
Directions: For each of the following questions, two quantities are given—one in Column A, the other in Column B. Compare the two quantities and mark your answer sheet as follows:

(A) if the quantity in Column A is greater

(B) if the quantity in Column B is greater

(C) if the quantities are equal

(D) if the relationship cannot be determined from the information given.
</td>
<td>
EXAMPLES
<table>
<tr><td>Column A</td><td>Column B</td></tr>
<tr><td colspan="2" align="center">a > 0
x > 0</td></tr>
</table>
E1.
<table>
<tr><td>a − x</td><td>a + x</td></tr>
</table>
Ⓐ ● Ⓒ Ⓓ
<hr>
E2.
<table>
<tr><td>The average of
17, 19, 21, 23</td><td>The average of
16, 18, 20, 22</td></tr>
</table>
● Ⓑ Ⓒ Ⓓ
</td>
</tr>
</table>

Notes: (1) Information concerning one or both of the compound quantities will be centered above the two columns for some items.
    (2) Symbols that appear in both columns represent the same thing in Column A as in Column B.
    (3) Letters such as *x*, *n*, and *k* are symbols for real numbers.

DO NOT MARK CHOICE (E) FOR THESE QUESTIONS. THERE ARE ONLY FOUR ANSWER CHOICES.

WHAT YOU SHOULD KNOW ABOUT QUANTITATIVE COMPARISONS

Quantitative comparisons test your knowledge of equal and unequal values and estimates. The more you know about the quantitative comparisons, the easier it is to handle them. Here are some tips on ways to approach them:

- There are special directions for quantitative comparisons. Make sure you take the time to understand them thoroughly.

- As you study the directions, memorize the four answer choices. They will stay the same for all quantitative comparison questions.

- You don't have to finish your calculations. Just reason far enough to determine which quantity is greater.

- If at least two answers are true, then the answer to that question is automatically D.

Shortcut. For the quantitative comparisons, reason the answer only to the point where you know which value is greater. Don't waste time actually finding the exact value.

No E! Make sure you never mark option E when responding to the four-choice quantitative comparison questions. There is no E.

EXAMPLES OF QUANTITATIVE COMPARISONS

Here are some examples of quantitative comparisons. Become familiar with them.

Example 9.1

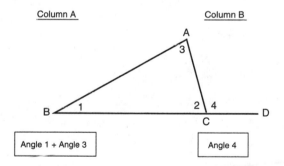

Column A   Column B

| Angle 1 + Angle 3 | Angle 4 |

Solution 9.1

Answer: C.

Here again you must remember some basic facts about geometry, but you don't have to necessarily remember the particular theorem that applies (an exterior angle of a triangle is equal to the sum of the two remote interior angles). You can see the theorem in the diagram. You can look at the diagram and see that Angles 1, 2, and 3 make up a triangle, which means that they add up to 180 degrees.

Angle 4 and Angle 2 equal a straight line, which equals 180 degrees. If you take Angle 2 out of each side, you see that Angle 1 + Angle 3 will equal Angle 4.

Example 9.2

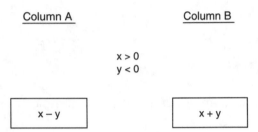

Column A

Column B

$x > 0$
$y < 0$

$x - y$

$x + y$

Solution 9.2

Answer: A.

In this case you can easily spot the fact that if you subtract a negative number it becomes positive, so x - y will be greater than x + y. But if you're unsure, plug in numbers.

Let's say that x = 5 and y = -2.

Therefore, x - y = 5 - (-2) = 5 + 2 = 7
and x + y = 5 + (-2) = 5 - 2 = 3

Example 9.3

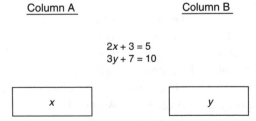

Column A

Column B

$2x + 3 = 5$
$3y + 7 = 10$

x

y

Solution 9.3

Answer: D.

Solution: Solve the two equations. $2x = 5 - 3 = 2$. So $x = 1$.

$3y = 10 - 7 = 3$. So $y = 1$.

Example 9.4

Column A	Column B
Number of seconds in one day	Number of minutes in April

Solution 9.4

Answer: A.

These questions usually require that you solve each side and then compare. Do so using estimates if necessary and try to avoid any long division or complex multiplication. If you see that you'll have to multiply or divide complex numbers, chances are that you can spot a relationship in the formula that makes the answer obvious without the arithmetic.

Solution: 60 seconds = 1 minute; 60 minutes = 1 hour; 24 hours= 1 day.

Seconds in 1 day = $60 \times 60 \times 24$

There are 30 days in April. Number of minutes in April = $60 \times 24 \times 30$, which is obviously less than the number of seconds in 1 day. No computation is even required.

Example 9.5

Column A	Column B
The average of 5 numbers is 20	
The sum of the five numbers	110

Solution 9.5

Answer: B.

If the average is 20, then the 5 numbers were added and the sum divided by 5 to give 20. The sum of these numbers must be 100.

Example 9.6

Column A	Column B
105% of 200	50% of 400

Solution 9.6

Answer: A.

105% of 200 is more than 200. 50% or one-half of 400 is 200.

SUMMARY

In this lesson you learned appropriate ways to approach quantitative comparisons.

10

FILLING IN THE GRID-INS

In this lesson you will become familiar with a new type of question on the SAT I, the "grid-in."

A new type of math question on the SAT I asks you to come up with and fill in your own answer, rather than choosing from multiple answers.

The grid-in questions (which are called "Student-Produced Responses" on the SAT I) are often no different from the regular multiple-choice questions. The difference is in the way you answer them. Grid-ins are closer to what you do in the classroom.

There are 10 grid-in questions on the SAT I.

Know Your Directions. Make sure you memorize the grid-in directions! You don't want to waste precious time on test day.

Here is what the grid-in looks like:

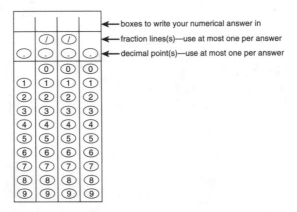

The answer grid for student-produced response questions is similar to the grid used for your zip code on the personal information section of your answer sheet.

GRID-IN RULES

- To enter an answer, you should write your answer in the upper boxes and then fill in the corresponding ovals directly underneath.

- The first row of ovals has only two ovals in the middle with "/". These allow you to enter numbers in fraction form.

- The second row of ovals is where you grid in decimal points.

- A horizontal bar separates the "/" and the decimal "." from the digits 0 to 9.

- Your answer can begin in any column.

- All answers to grid-in questions are positive numbers.

- No answer requires more than four columns.

- If a question has more than one correct answer, grid either one of them, but *not* both.

- You can use either decimals or fractions to express your answer.

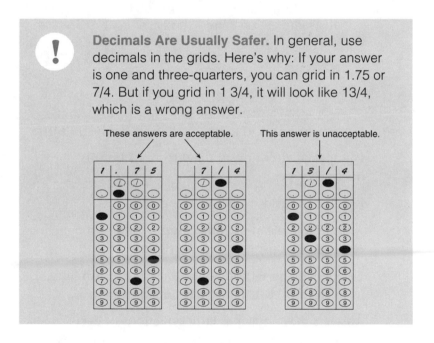

Decimals Are Usually Safer. In general, use decimals in the grids. Here's why: If your answer is one and three-quarters, you can grid in 1.75 or 7/4. But if you grid in 1 3/4, it will look like 13/4, which is a wrong answer.

These answers are acceptable.   This answer is unacceptable.

When you round off a decimal answer, be sure to use all the available grid spaces so that you have the "most accurate" answer (the answer 2/3 can be .666 or .667. But it *cannot* be .67 or .7).

Upper Boxes Don't Count. Only answers that are recorded in the ovals will be counted, regardless of whether you have filled in the upper boxes.

 Go Ahead and Guess. You *don't* lose any points for a wrong answer here. So if you think your answer might be correct, grid it in.

GRID-IN TIPS

Here are some quick tips to help you do well on the grid-ins:

- Pay special attention to the directions on this question type.

- Practice the grid-ins before test day.

- Although you can use any column, grid in the result either flush left or flush right.

- Decide which method you will use (i.e., flush left or flush right) before test day and stick to it.

- Answers may appear as either fractions or decimals: For example, you can grid three-quarters as either 3/4 or .75.

- If your answer is a repeating decimal, grid as much of it as you can fit in the grid. If you need to round a repeating decimal, round only the last digit.

- Be especially careful to avoid careless errors, since you don't have choices provided. Check and re-check your calculations and answers.

- Do a quick check to make sure your answer looks right.

- Be aware that some grid-in questions have more than one correct answer.

- If your answer is zero, just enter 0 in any column (other than column 1, where no 0 appears).

- Mark only one oval in any column. If you change your answer, erase the old response thoroughly.

- Use your calculator whenever you think you may make a mistake doing a calculation by hand. After reasoning correctly, you don't want to get an answer wrong because you made a mistake in your calculation.

- No question will have a negative answer.

- Leave unused columns blank.

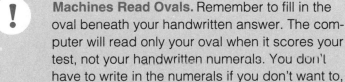

Machines Read Ovals. Remember to fill in the oval beneath your handwritten answer. The computer will read only your oval when it scores your test, not your handwritten numerals. You don't have to write in the numerals if you don't want to, but doing so can help prevent mistakes.

EXAMPLES OF GRID-IN QUESTIONS

Now let's look at some practice questions.

Example 10.1

If there are 30 students at a meeting of the Forum Club, and 20 are wearing white, 17 are wearing black, and 14 are wearing both black and white, how many are wearing neither black nor white?

Solution 10.1

Solution: The easiest way to arrive at the solution is by using two overlapping circles.

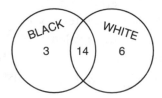

This accounts for 23 students, leaving 7, which is the answer you must grid in.

Example 10.2

If a ❑ b means (a × b) + (a - b), find the value of 4 ❑ 2

Solution 10.2

4 ❑ 2 = (4 × 2) + (4 - 2) = 8 + 2 = 10. You must grid in the answer 10.

Example 10.3

How many 2-inch squares are needed to fill a border around the edge of the shaded square with a side of 6 inches, as shown in the figure below?

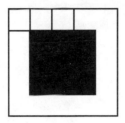

Solution 10.3

The answer you must grid in is 16.

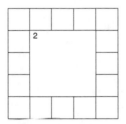

Impossible Answers. No grid-in answer will be a negative number or a number above 9999. If you get an answer that does not fit in the grid, you've made a mistake.

Example 10.4

What is the ratio of 6 minutes to 6 hours?

Solution 10.4

$$\frac{6 \text{ minutes}}{6 \text{ hours}} = \frac{6 \text{ minutes}}{6(60) \text{ minutes}} = \frac{1}{60.}$$ You must grid in 1/60.

Example 10.5

$\sqrt{7+9+7+9+7+9+7+9} =$

Solution 10.5

$\sqrt{7+9+7+9+7+9+7+9} =$

$\sqrt{4(7+9)} =$

$\sqrt{4(16)} =$

$\sqrt{64} = 8.$

You must grid in the answer 8.

SUMMARY

In this lesson you were introduced to the new "grid-in" type questions and learned the rules for filling in your grid-in answers.

USING CALCULATORS

In this lesson you will learn guidelines for using calculators on the SAT I.

You can use calculators while taking the SAT I. No question requires you to use a calculator, but if you have one and know how to use it, you should bring your calculator with you to the test center.

TIPS ON USING A CALCULATOR

The most important point to remember about using a calculator is not to use it blindly. First decide whether or not a question needs a calculator to find the answer. If you try to use a calculator on each question without thinking, you could actually lose valuable time. Here are some other tips to help you use calculators effectively:

- Bring a calculator only if you are used to using one in the classroom or at home, and bring only that model.

- Don't buy a new, sophisticated calculator, hoping that it will help you do better on the test. It will only make you nervous.

- Don't expect to use another student's calculator during the test. You won't be allowed to share calculators.

- Make sure your calculator has fresh batteries. If it fails during the test, you must continue without it.

- Practice taking sample tests using your calculator.

Calculators that Are Not Allowed. You can use almost any type or brand of calculator *except* the following: handheld minicomputers or laptop computers; electronic writing pads or pen-input devices; pocket organizers; calculators with keyboards where the top row spells QWERTY; calculators with paper tape or printers; calculators that talk; and calculators that need an external power source such as an outlet.

SUMMARY

In this lesson you learned that you can use a calculator on the SAT I, some tips about using calculators, and the types of calculators that you can and cannot use.

12

PRACTICING FOR THE BIG EVENT

In this lesson you will learn the best ways to practice for the SAT.

TAKE THE PSAT/NMSQT

Taking the Preliminary SAT/NMSQT is by far the best way to practice for the SAT I. There are two main reasons:

1. You get the opportunity to take a shorter version of the SAT I.

2. You take a similar test under actual test conditions.

If you haven't already taken the PSAT/NMSQT, ask your guidance counselor for more information about how to register for it.

TAKE A FULL-LENGTH PRACTICE SAT I

A second way to practice for the SAT I is to take full-length practice tests. Visit a bookstore and you'll quickly see that there are many test-preparation guides on the shelves. Choose a publication or software that will provide you with several practice tests. A scaled-down version of a full-length SAT exam appears in Appendix C.

Remember, part of getting ready to take the SAT I is getting used to what it will feel like when you take the real thing. So, try simulating the test day. Get up early on a Saturday morning, set aside 2 1/2 hours of uninterrupted time, and practice taking the test while timing yourself with an alarm clock. Use a calculator if you are comfortable using one.

The practice test will give you a good idea of what to expect on the actual test.

This Test Is Different. The SAT test you eventually take will probably be different from the practice tests. For one thing, the sections may be in a different order. The actual SAT I will also include a seventh section, called the "equating" section, that doesn't count toward your score. This section is not included in the practice tests.

SOME WORDS ABOUT SAT PREP COURSES

Many organizations offer SAT coaching courses to help students prepare for the SAT.

Whether or not to take a course is really up to you; it depends on how you like to learn. Some students prefer to work independently with books, videos, or software; others prefer a group setting with an instructor present.

Coaching Can't "Up" Your Score. There are no shortcuts that can make up for years of academic study. But you can't just go into the test cold and expect to do your best. You must prepare in some way.

If you do choose to take a course, just be leery of any course that claims extremely high score gains—especially if you are being asked to pay hundreds of dollars for it. Your score might improve after taking such a course, and then again it might not. When considering a coaching course, first ask your guidance counselor if any SAT test preparation classes are being offered at your high school; these courses are usually considerably cheaper than commercial courses and often offer an excellent review of the material. Some do not, however—particularly those that are just a couple of quick sessions that give you an overview of the test itself.

Keep in mind that the SAT I tests reasoning skills that have been developed over years of schooling. You can't expect to remember everything with just a cursory review of the material covered. The only real way to up your SAT score is through solid preparation.

Do I or Don't I? If taking a course over many weeks or months, with an instructor, class discussion, and practice tests, is the way you prepare best, that's great. If you can study on your own over that same period of time, using the many excellent materials that are available (including taking practice tests under simulated test conditions), then you'll probably up your score just as much.

SUMMARY

In this lesson you learned that one of the most important ways to prepare for the SAT is by taking practice tests.

13

NOW THAT IT'S ALL OVER

In this lesson you will learn what steps to take after the SAT is over, how it is scored, how you can find out more about your performance on the test, and ways to improve if you take it again.

RIGHT AFTER THE TEST

First, breathe a sigh of relief. Then, congratulate yourself on getting through it and do something fun. But whatever you do, don't beat yourself up for how you think you did. If you really think you bombed, you can take the test again (and again), as many times as you want until you feel comfortable. Or, if you feel you did the very best you could on your first try, forget about it and move on with your life.

THE ENVELOPE, PLEASE

About five to six weeks after you take the SAT I, you will receive your score report in the mail. You will receive two scores:

one for verbal and one for math. These scores range from 200 to 800, with 800 being the best score. If you requested it when you registered, a score report will also be sent to the colleges and scholarship programs you indicated. If you gave your high school code, your high school will also get a copy.

Recentering. In April 1995, scores began to be reported on a "recentered" score scale. If you took SAT tests both before and after April 1, 1995, you will notice that some scores are on the original scale and some are on the recentered scale. For help comparing scores reported on the different scales, see your guidance counselor.

On this report you will get your score range, which is typically between 30 points below and 30 points above your actual numerical score. This will help you pinpoint where your scores are likely to fall if you take the test several times. College admission officers know this and consider the range as well as your score to assess your performance.

PERCENTILES

Your score report will also give you a percentile score, which compares your scores to the scores of others who have taken the test. The percentile is a number between 1 and 99, and it indicates what percentage of students scored lower than you did. For example, if your percentile is 75, it means that out of every 100 test takers in the comparison group, you performed better than 75 of them.

SAT I Services

On your score report you will also see how you did on each part of the test. The Educational Testing Service offers additional score analyses to students who want to check their answers and examine their test performance. You can order these services when you register to take the test or after you receive your score report. (Ordering information will come with the score report.) Use these information services to analyze your strengths and weaknesses with an eye toward improvement.

Through the *Question-and-Answer Service*, you can order a copy of the sections of the test you took, your answers, a list of the correct answers, and information about the types of questions and difficulty level of each question.

The *Student Answer Service* can tell you how you answered each question (correctly, incorrectly, or left blank), the difficulty level of each question, and an indication of each type of question. It does not provide an opportunity to order a copy of your answer sheet and does not include a copy of the questions themselves, the way the Question-and-Answer Service does.

To find out which service to order, consult the *SAT Program Registration Bulletin,* which should be in your guidance counselor's office.

Take Inventory

Whether you did great or not so great, it's a good idea to take inventory and zero in on things you can improve. Here are six questions to ask yourself:

1. Did I know the directions or did I have to waste valuable time rereading them?

2. Did I have enough time to finish all the sections?

3. Did I go too fast?

4. Did I panic? If I did, how did I regain control?

5. Did I make errors because I didn't read the question correctly and missed key words or ideas?

6. Did I conquer the test, or did it conquer me?

THE SAT AND COLLEGE ADMISSION

If you are an American student, you are very lucky. Most colleges in this country use SAT scores as just one variable of several in evaluating your candidacy for admission. In many foreign countries, test scores *do* make or break a student's chance to get a quality education. You, on the other hand, have many choices before you; it is never a one-shot deal. Even if you get terrible scores and don't get into the college of your choice (or if you get good scores and still don't get in), if you keep trying you will get into a college somewhere. Whichever college you attend, you can always distinguish yourself once you get there.

SUMMARY

In this lesson you learned what to do after the test is over, how the test is scored, how you can find out more about your performance, and some ways you can improve next time.

APPENDIX A

WORDS TO KNOW FOR THE SAT I

A good knowledge of vocabulary will help you answer verbal analogies, sentence completion questions, and the critical reading questions. So vocabulary building is important in preparing for the test.

Although trying to come up with a definitive list of vocabulary words to know for the SAT I is impossible, here are some words designed to give you additional practice for the test. Pick 15 to 20 new words to learn at a time from the following list. Make up flash cards or write them on a piece of paper you can carry with you.

aberration (noun) Deviation from what is correct or right.

accolade (noun) Embrace; award; commendation.

acerbic (adj) Bitter; harsh; caustic.

acute (adj) 1. Perceptive. 2. Excruciating.

admonish (verb) Caution; reprove mildly; reprimand.

adroit (adj) Dexterous; proficient; skillful.

adulterate (verb) Make impure or inferior by adding improper ingredients; contaminate; pollute.

advocate (verb) 1. Argue for a cause; defend. 2. Support; uphold.

alacrity (noun) Eagerness; zeal; speed.

altruistic (adj) Concerned about the general welfare of others; charitable; generous.

amiable (adj) Cordial; of pleasant disposition; friendly.

ascetic (adj) Strict; austere.

audacity (noun) Boldness or adventurousness; gall.

avarice (noun) Extreme desire for wealth; greed; acquisitiveness.

balm (noun) Soothing ointment for pain or healing; salve.

banal (adj) Trite; insipid; ordinary.

bane (noun) Deadly affliction; curse; plague.

belittle (verb) Humiliate; tease; diminish in importance.

bemused (adj) Preoccupied by thought; bewildered; perplexed.

blithe (adj) Happy; pleased; delighted.

boisterous (adj) Noisy; loud; violent; rowdy.

brevity (noun) Briefness; succinctness; terseness.

callow (adj) Inexperienced; immature; naïve.

carouse (verb) Drink to excess; live it up.

clamor (noun) Loud noise or complaint; commotion; din.

clandestine (adj) Furtive; surreptitious; secret.

clemency (noun) Lenience; mercy; compassion.

coercion (noun) Intimidation; duress; force; compulsion.

conjugal (adj) Matrimonial; nuptial; marital.

constrict (verb) Squeeze; pinch; obstruct; block.

contrite (adj) Penitent; apologetic; remorseful.

credulous (adj) Gullible; unsuspecting; naïve.

cryptic (adj) Enigmatic; obscure; secret; puzzling.

debased (adj) Lowered in status or character; degenerate.

decipher (verb) Solve or figure out a puzzle; translate; untangle.

decorum (noun) Appropriate conduct; polite or proper behavior, protocol.

depravity (noun) Perverted disposition; wickedness; vileness; corruption.

desecrate (verb) Contaminate; profane; defile.

desolate (adj) Alone; without hope or comfort; forsaken.

diatribe (noun) Extreme, bitter, and abusive speech; vituperation; tirade.

diffidence (noun) Self-doubt; timidity; shyness.

diligent (adj) Assiduous; studious; hard-working.

disaffected (adj) Disillusioned; dissatisfied; discontented.

disband (verb) Disperse; dissipate; scatter; dispel.

discontent (adj) Unhappy; displeased; miserable.

dishearten (verb) Dismay; daunt; depress.

disparage (verb) Deprecate; belittle or abuse.

dissemble (verb) Disguise; conceal; mask; camouflage.

dissension (noun) Conflict; disagreement; strife.

dissonant (adj) Cacophonous; inharmonious; discordant; strident.

dissuade (verb) Obstruct; hinder; deter.

divination (noun) Prediction; prophecy; forecast.

duplicity (noun) Cunning; fraud; trickery; deception.

edify (verb) Instruct; enlighten; educate.

efface (verb) Cancel; delete; obliterate.

elucidate (verb) Interpret; define; clarify; explain.

emanate (verb) Radiate; flow from; emit.

empathize (verb) Identify with; understand.

emulate (verb) Model; pattern.

enervate (verb) Exhaust or weaken; debilitate.

enigmatic (adj) Cryptic; baffling; mysterious.

ennui (noun) Dullness; boredom; monotony.

enthrall (verb) Mesmerize; captivate; thrill.

ephemeral (adj) Transitory; fleeting; passing; temporary.

equilibrium (noun) Balance; stability; poise.

erudition (noun) Learning; knowledge; enlightenment.

esoteric (adj) Confidential; personal; private; privileged.

expedite (verb) Speed up matters; accelerate; quicken.

fallible (adj) Faulty; imperfect.

fastidious (adj) Meticulous; exacting.

fathom (verb) Measure; discover; perceive.

fetid (adj) Possessing an offensive smell; malodorous; foul; gamey.

foible (noun) Frailty; imperfection; weakness.

fume (noun) Gas; vapor; harmful or irritating smoke.

furtive (adj) Clandestine; secretive; surreptitious; covert.

garble (verb) Confuse; scramble; distort.

garish (adj) Gaudy; ostentatious; excessive.

garner (verb) Collect; receive; attain; acquire.

grovel (verb) Act in a servile way; cringe; kneel.

guile (noun) Wiliness; deceit; cunning.

hackneyed (adj) Trite; common; overdone; banal.

hallow (verb) Make holy; consecrate; sanctify.

harbor (verb) Preserve; conceal; secure; shelter.

haughty (adj) Arrogant; disdainful; blatantly proud; contemptuous.

histrionic (adj) Pertaining to actors; melodramatic.

hyperbole (noun) Exaggeration; fanciful statement; enhancement.

immutable (adj) Incorruptible; enduring; unchanging.

impervious (adj) Airtight; sealed; impenetrable.

impetuous (adj) Hasty; rash; impulsive.

inauspicious (adj) Unfavorable.

incisive (adj) Perceptive; astute.

incoherent (adj) Illogical; inconsistent.

incorrigible (adj) Unruly; delinquent; incapable of reform.

indecorous (adj) Inappropriate; indelicate; unseemly.

indefatigable (adj) Diligent; persistent; inexhaustible.

indolence (noun) Lethargy; idleness; sloth.

ingenuous (adj) Genuine; open; candid; frank.

innocuous (adj) Dull; harmless; innocent.

inscrutable (adj) Mysterious; perplexing.

insipid (adj) Dull; banal; tasteless.

irascible (adj) Testy; touchy; irritable.

judicious (adj) Logical; reasonable; clever.

kinetic (adj) Caused by motion; dynamic.

labyrinth (noun) Maze; network; puzzle.

lamentation (noun) Complaint; moan.

languish (verb) Decline; diminish; weaken.

laudable (adj) Commendable; admirable; exemplary.

lethargy (noun) Idleness; listlessness; passivity.

levity (noun) Lightness; frivolity.

lithe (adj) Flexible; agile; mobile; bendable.

lurid (adj) Shockingly vivid; horrifying; sensational.

malevolent (adj) Venomous; spiteful; malignant.

meticulous (adj) Precise; scrupulous; particular.

mundane (adj) Boring; ordinary; typical; tedious.

nadir (noun) Lowest point.

naïve (adj) Foolishly simple; childlike.

nebulous (adj) Unclear; vague; indefinite.

nefarious (adj) Evil; vile; sinister; wicked.

noxious (adj) Harmful; malignant.

odious (adj) Detestable; loathsome; revolting; sickening.

officious (adj) Meddlesome.

opaque (adj) Impenetrable by light; dull; dark; obscure.

opulent (adj) Affluent; well-to-do; plentiful.

ostentatious (adj) Conspicuous; showy.

ostracize (verb) Exclude; isolate; bar; shun.

palpable (adj) Noticeable; obvious; apparent.

paltry (adj) Minor; petty; insignificant.

partisan (noun) Fan or supporter; enthusiast supporting a particular cause or issue.

paucity (noun) Scarcity; shortage; dearth.

pedantic (adj) Stuffy or dogmatic; meticulous; academic.

peripheral (adj) Marginal; outer; surrounding.

platitude (noun) 1. Triteness. 2. Cliché; trivial remark.

pliable (adj) Limber; malleable; flexible.

poignant (adj) Intense; powerful; biting; piercing.

precocious (adj) Showing premature development.

precursor (noun) Forerunner.

primeval (adj) Belonging to a primitive age.

procrastinate (verb) Postpone; stall; defer.

proficient (adj) Skillful; masterful; expert.

progeny (noun) Heir; descendant; offspring.

prolific (adj) Fruitful; abundant; fertile.

prosaic (adj) Common; routine; ordinary.

quandary (noun) Dilemma; mire; entanglement.

querulous (adj) Difficult; testy; disagreeable.

rabid (adj) Berserk; diseased; sick.

rancorous (adj) Antagonistic; hostile; spiteful.

raucous (adj) Harsh; annoying; piercing; shrill.

recalcitrant (adj) Headstrong; disobedient; stubborn.

redundant (adj) Excessive; repetitious; unnecessary.

regimen (noun) Administration; government; system.

resilient (adj) Elastic; stretchy; rebounding.

resonant (adj) Reverberant; ringing.

resplendent (adj) Dazzling; glorious; intense.

restive (adj) Nervous; restless; uneasy.

reverent (adj) Devout; solemn; worshipful.

rudiment (noun) Beginning; foundation or source.

ruminate (verb) Contemplate; think about.

spurious (adj) Bogus; false.

squalor (noun) 1. Severe poverty. 2. Filthiness.

stratagem (noun) Plot; tactic; deception.

strident (adj) Discordant; harsh; piercing.

strife (noun) Conflict; turmoil; struggle.

surfeit (noun) Overabundance; excess; surplus.

svelte (adj) Graceful; slim.

taciturn (adj) Reserved; shy; uncommunicative.

tawdry (adj) Gaudy; showy; loud.

temerity (noun) Rashness; audacity; recklessness.

tenuous (adj) Attenuated; flimsy; thin.

tirade (noun) Diatribe; angry speech.

unfathomable (adj) Baffling; puzzling; incomprehensible.

unscathed (adj) Unhurt; uninjured.

unwieldy (adj) Clumsy; awkward; unmanageable.

vacillate (verb) Hedge; waver; fluctuate.

vehement (adj) Fierce; emphatic; intense.

venerate (verb) Admire; show respect.

veracity (noun) Truth; sincerity; honesty; candor.

verdant (adj) Lush; thick with vegetation; leafy.

viable (adj) Living; alive; feasible.

vigilance (noun) Attentiveness; prudence; care.

vilify (verb) Defame; denigrate.

voluminous (adj) Huge; immense; bulky.

voracious (adj) 1. Enthusiastic; overly eager. 2. Starving.

writhe (verb) Squirm; twist.

zealot (noun) Fanatic; radical; enthusiast.

zenith (noun) Apex; summit; peak.

BASIC MATH RULES TO KNOW FOR THE SAT I

ARITHMETIC OPERATIONS

Addition (2 + 2 = 4)

Subtraction (4 - 2 = 2)

Multiplication (2 × 2 = 4)

Division (4 ÷ 2 = 2)

Raising to a power (2^2) = 4

Finding a square root ($\sqrt{2}$)

Finding a cube root ($^3\sqrt{2}$)

PROPERTIES OF NUMBERS

Even + Even = Even (Even - Even = Even)

Even + Odd = Odd (Even - Odd = Odd)

Odd + Even = Odd (Odd - Even = Odd)

Odd + Odd = Even (Odd - Odd = Even)

Even × Even = Even

Even × Odd = Even

Odd × Even = Even

Odd × Odd = Odd

Positive × Positive = Positive

Positive ÷ Positive = Positive

Positive × Negative = Negative
(Negative × Positive = Negative)

Positive ÷ Negative = Negative
(Negative ÷ Positive = Negative)

Negative × Negative = Positive

Negative ÷ Negative = Positive

MATHEMATICAL DEFINITIONS

- *Prime numbers* are numbers that can be evenly divided only by themselves and 1. Examples: 2, 3, 5, 7, 11, 13, 17, 19, 23, and 29.

- *Composite numbers* are the opposite of prime numbers. Composite numbers can be divided without a remainder by numbers other than themselves and 1. Examples: 4, 6, 8, 9, 10, 12, 14, 15, 16, 18.

- *Whole numbers* include 0 and any positive multiple of 1.

- *Integers* are 0 and any positive or negative whole number. Consecutive integers are integers listed in increasing order: -1, 0, 1, 2, and so forth.

Symbols Used

= means equal to

≠ means not equal to

< means less than

> means greater than

≤ means less than or equal to

≥ means greater than or equal to

Fractions and Decimals

- Fractions and decimals become larger when added but smaller when multiplied.

- Fractions and decimals become smaller when subtracted but larger when divided.

- To convert a decimal to a percentage, move the decimal point two places to the right.
  Example: 0.25 = 25%.

- To convert a percentage into a decimal, move the decimal point two places to the left.
  Example: 25% = 0.25.

- A fraction is a part of a whole. Think of it this way: 2 is one-half of 4.

- To convert a fraction to a decimal, divide the top number (the numerator) by the bottom number (the denominator). Example: $^3/_4 = 3 \div 4 = .75$

ANGLES

- The number of degrees of the arc in a circle is 360.

- The measure of degrees in a straight angle is 180.

- The number of degrees in a right angle is 90.

- When parallel lines are cut by a third line:

    all the large angles are equal

    all the small angles are equal

    any big plus any small angle equals 180 degrees

- The sum of the measures of the interior angles of a triangle is 180 degrees.

- The sum of degrees of the interior angles of a polygon of N sides is 180(N - 2).

TRIANGLES

- Within a triangle, if two angles are equal the lengths of their opposite sides are equal.

- In a right triangle, the square of the longest side (the hypotenuse) is equal to the sum of the squares of the other two sides.

- In a triangle with angles of 45°, 45°, and 90°, the length of the hypotenuse is equal to the length of either side multiplied by $\sqrt{2}$, and each of the sides is equal to $1/2$ times the length of the hypotenuse times $\sqrt{2}$.

- An equilateral triangle (three equal sides) has three 60° angles. A triangle with three equal angles is equilateral.

- The area of a triangle is equal to $1/2$ times the altitude times the base.

RECTANGLES AND SQUARES

- The perimeter of a rectangle is equal to the sum of the lengths of the four sides.

- The area of a rectangle is equal to the width × the length.

- The diagonal of a rectangle is the hypotenuse of a right triangle with sides that are the width and length of the rectangle.

PRACTICE SAT MINI-EXAM

The following exam is a scaled-down version of a full-length SAT exam. The exam is divided into six sections. Before beginning each section, be sure to review the directions and tips listed for that section in the corresponding lesson in this book. If you would like to replicate actual SAT test-taking conditions, you should time yourself and allow yourself only the time allotted for each section.

An answer key and explanatory answers are provided beginning on page 127.

Please note that an answer sheet and grids for the Student-Produced Response Questions are not provided here.

SECTION 1

10 Questions • Time—10 Minutes

1. An audience that laughs in all the wrong places can_____even the most experienced actor.

   (A) disparage

   (B) allay

   (C) disconcert

   (D) upbraid

   (E) satiate

2. Their assurances of good faith were hollow; they_____on the agreement almost at once.

   (A) conferred

   (B) expiated

   (C) recapitulated

   (D) obtruded

   (E) reneged

3. If we _____ our different factions, then together we can gain the majority in their legislature.

(A) amalgamate

(B) manifest

(C) preclude

(D) alienate

(E) deviate

4. THROAT : SWALLOW ::

(A) teeth : chew

(B) eyelid : wink

(C) nose : point

(D) ear : absorb

(E) mouth : smile

5. GARNET : RED ::

(A) pearl : round

(B) diamond : solid

(C) emerald : green

(D) ivory : lining

(E) silver : shining

6. PATIENCE : VIRTUES ::

(A) prudence : skills

(B) sailing : crafts

(C) grief : traits

(D) temerity : vices

(E) literature : arts

Questions 7–10 are based on the following passage.

One of the most frequently read political treatises of all time is The Prince *by Niccolò Machiavelli (1469–1527). The word* Machiavellian *is used to mean diabolical, but Machiavelli's work, although sometimes used to justify dictatorship, is thoughtful, original, and often brilliant.*

> *I say that every Prince should desire to be accounted*
> *merciful and not cruel. Nevertheless, he should be*
> *on his guard against the abuse of this quality of mercy.*
> *Cesare Borgia was reputed cruel, yet his cruelty restored*
> (5) *Romagna, united it, and brought it to order and*
> *obedience; so that if we look at things in their true light,*
> *it will be seen that he was in reality far more merciful*
> *than the people of Florence, who, to avoid the*
> *imputation of cruelty, suffered Pistoja to be torn to pieces*
> (10) *by factions.*

A Prince should therefore disregard that reproach of being thought cruel where it enables him to keep his subjects united and obedient. For he who quells disorder by a very few signal examples will in the end be more
(15)   merciful than he who from too great leniency permits things to take their course and so to result in rapine and bloodshed; for these hurt the whole State, whereas the severities of the Prince injure individuals only.

And for a new Prince, of all others, it is impossible
(20)   to escape a name for cruelty, since new States are full of dangers. Wherefore Virgil, by the mouth of Dido, excuses the harshness of her reign on the plea that it was new, saying:

A fate unkind, and newness in my reign

(25)   Compel me thus to guard a wide domain.

Nevertheless, the new Prince should not be too ready of belief, nor too easily set in motion; nor should he himself be the first to raise alarms; but should so temper prudence with kindliness that too great confidence in
(30)   others shall not throw him off his guard, nor groundless distrust render him insupportable.

And here comes the question whether it is better to be loved rather than be feared, or feared rather than be loved. It might perhaps be answered that we should wish
(35)   to be both; but since love and fear can hardly exist together, if we must choose between them, it is far safer to be feared than loved. For of men it may generally be affirmed that they are thankless, fickle, false, studious to avoid danger, greedy of gain, devoted to you while you
(40)   are able to confer benefits upon them, and ready, as I said before, while danger is distant, to shed their blood, and sacrifice their property, their lives, and their children for you; but in the hour of need they turn against you.

The Prince, therefore, who without otherwise securing
(45)   *himself builds wholly on their professions is undone. For*
the friendships which we buy with a price, and do not
gain by greatness and nobility of character, though they
may be fairly earned are not made good, but fail us when
we have occasion to use them.

7. Cesare Borgia (line 4) is held up as an example of

(A) an unnecessarily cruel Prince

(B) someone who drew strength from cruel actions

(C) a leader loved by his people and feared by foreigners

(D) a compassionate man with a bad reputation

(E) a model of obedience and duty

8. "A very few signal examples" (line 14) would most likely imply

(A) commutations of sentences

(B) censures

(C) fines

(D) executions

(E) imprisonments

9. The main point of paragraph 4 seems to be that a Prince

(A) cannot escape being cruel

(B) is in constant danger of being unseated

(C) should not trust anyone

(D) needs to be kind to his subjects

(E) must balance trust with caution

10. Machiavelli asserts in this passage that

(A) the people of Florence overreacted cruelly against Pistoja

(B) Cesare Borgia was just as cruel as the people of Florence

(C) the subjects of a ruler remain loyal to him only as long as he continues to make them happy

(D) it is better to be loved than feared

(E) fear without love is better than love without fear

Section 2

8 Questions • Time—10 Minutes

1. One angle of a triangle is 82°. The other two angles are in the ratio 2 : 5. Find the number of degrees in the smallest angle on the triangle.

(A) 14

(B) 25

(C) 28

(D) 38

(E) 82

2. Village A has a population of 6,800, which is decreasing at a rate of 120 per year. Village B has a population of 4,200, which is increasing at a rate of 80 per year. In how many years will the population of the two villages be equal?

(A) 9

(B) 11

(C) 13

(D) 14

(E) 16

3. If $*x$ is defined such that $*x=x^2-2x$, the value of $*2-*1$ is

(A) −1

(B) 0

(C) 1

(D) 2

(E) 4

4. In a right triangle, the ratio of the legs is 1 : 2. If the area of the triangle is 25 square units, what is the length of the hypotenuse?

(A) $\sqrt{5}$

(B) $5\sqrt{5}$

(C) $5\sqrt{3}$

(D) $10\sqrt{3}$

(E) $25\sqrt{3}$

5. In the graph below, the axes and the origin are not shown. If point P has coordinates (3,7), what are the coordinates of point Q, assuming each box is one unit?

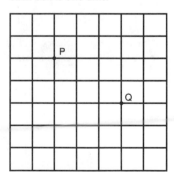

(A) (5,6)

(B) (1,10)

(C) (6,9)

(D) (6,5)

(E) (5,10)

6. If $r=5x$, how many tenths of r does $\frac{1}{2}$ of x equal?

(A) 1

(B) 2

(C) 3

(D) 4

(E) 5

8. In any square, the length of one side is

(A) one-half the diagonal of the square

(B) the square root of the perimeter of the square

(C) about .7 the length of the diagonal of the square

(D) the square root of the diagonal

(E) one-fourth the area

7. ABCD is a parallelogram, and DE=EC.

What is the ratio of triangle ADE to the area of the parallelogram?

(A) 2 : 5

(B) 1 : 2

(C) 1 : 3

(D) 1 : 4

(E) It cannot be determined from the information given.

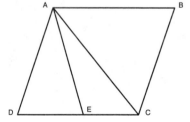

Section 3

4 Questions • Time—5 Minutes

Questions 1–4 are based on the following passages.

Writing in eighteenth-century England, essayist William Shen-stone and his more famous compatriot, Horace Walpole, spent some time preoccupied with the question of good taste in landscape architecture.

Passage 1—William Shenstone, from "Unconnected Thoughts on Gardening" (1764)

The eye should always look down upon water: customary nature makes this requisite. I know nothing more sensibly displeasing than Mr. T—'s flat ground twixt terrace and his water.

(5) *It is not easy to account for the fondness of former times for straight-lined avenues to their houses; straight-lined walks through their woods; and, in short, every kind of straight line where the foot is to travel over what the eye has done before. This circumstance is one*
(10) *objection. Another, somewhat of the same kind, is the repetition of the same object, tree after tree for a length of way together. . . . To stand still and survey such avenues may afford some slender satisfaction through the change derived from perspective; but to move on continually and*
(15) *find no change of scene in the last attendant on our change of place must give actual pain to a person of taste. For such an one to be condemned to pass along the famous vista from Moscow to Petersburg or that other from Agra to Lahore in India, must be as disagreeable a*
(20) *sentence as to be condemned to labor at the galleys. I conceive some ideas of the sensation he must feel from walking but a few minutes, immured, betwixt Lord D—'s*

high shorn yew hedges, which run exactly parallel at a
distance of about ten feet and are contrived perfectly to
(25)   exclude all kinds of objects whatsoever.

When a building or other object has been once
viewed from its proper point, the foot should never travel
to it by the same path which the eye has traveled over
before. Lose the object, and draw nigh obliquely. . .

(30)   Water should ever appear as an irregular lake or
winding stream.

Passage 2—Horace Walpole, from "Essay on Modern Gardening" (1771)

. . . At that moment appeared Kent, painter enough to
taste the charms of the landscape, bold and opinionative
enough to dare and to dictate, and born with a genius to
(5)   strike out a great system from the twilight of imperfect
essays. He leaped the fence, and saw that all nature was
a garden. He felt the delicious contrast of hill and valley,
changing imperceptibly into each other, tasted the beauty
of the gentle swell or concave scoop, and remarked how
(10)   loose groves crowned an easy eminence with happy
ornament, and while they called in the distant view
between their graceful stems, removed and extended the
perspective by delusive comparison.

Thus the pencil of his imagination bestowed all the
(15)   arts of landscape on the scenes he handled. The great
principles on which he worked were perspective, and light
and shade. Groups of trees broke too uniform or too
extensive a lawn; evergreens and woods were opposed to
the glare of the champaign, and where the view was less
(20)   fortunate, or so much exposed as to be beheld at once, he
blotted out some parts by thick shades, to divide it into

variety, or to make the richest scene more enchanting by reserving it to a farther advance of the spectator's steps. Thus. . .he realized the compositions of the greatest masters in painting. Where objects were wanting to

(25)   *animate his horizon, his taste as an architect could bestow immediate termination. His buildings, his seats, his temples were more the works of his pencil than of his compasses. We owe the restoration of Greece and the diffusion of architecture to his skill in landscape.*

(30)   *But of all the beauties he added to the face of this beautiful country, none surpassed his management of water. Adieu to canals, circular basins, and cascades tumbling down marble steps, that last absurd magnificence of Italian and French villas. The forced*

(35)   *elevation of cataracts was no more. The gentle stream was taught to serpentize seemingly at its pleasure, and where discontinued by different levels, its course appeared to be concealed by thickets properly interspersed, and glittered again at a distance where it*

(40)   *might be supposed naturally to arrive. Its borders were smoothed, but preserved their waving irregularity. A few trees scattered here and there on its edges sprinkled the tame bank that accompanied its meanders; and when it disappeared among the hills, shades descending from the*

(45)   *heights leaned towards its progress, and framed the distant point of light under which it was lost, as it turned aside to either hand of the blue horizon.*

1. The phrase *sensibly displeasing* in Passage 1 (line 3) is used to mean

   (A) rationally provoking

   (B) reasonably unpleasant

   (C) wisely disturbing

   (D) nonsensically pleasing

   (E) annoying to the senses

2. How does the author of Passage 1 feel about straight lines?

   (A) They are painfully boring.

   (B) They are necessary evils.

   (C) They are used to good effect in India.

   (D) They are satisfyingly attractive.

   (E) They are appropriate for the banks of steams.

3. The word *serpentize* (line 36) in Passage 2 seems to mean

   (A) shed

   (B) poison

   (C) hiss

   (D) twist

   (E) drop

4. How do both authors feel about water in parks?

   (A) The eye should look down on it.

   (B) It should be used sparingly.

   (C) It should look natural.

   (D) It should follow straight lines.

   (E) It should be lined with trees.

Section 4

3 Questions • Time—5 Minutes

1. Which one of the following quantities has the lowest numerical value?

(A) $\frac{4}{5}$

(B) $\frac{7}{9}$

(C) .76

(D) $\frac{5}{7}$

(E) $\frac{9}{11}$

2. A salesperson earns twice as much in December as in each of the other months of a year. What part of this salesperson's entire year's earnings are earned in December?

(A) $\frac{1}{7}$

(B) $\frac{2}{13}$

(C) $\frac{1}{6}$

(D) $\frac{2}{11}$

(E) $\frac{3}{14}$

3. If x=−1, then $3x+2x+x+1=$

(A) −5

(B) −1

(C) 1

(D) 2

(E) 5

SECTION 5

11 Questions • Time—10 Minutes

1. The_____was greatest when the pitcher paused before delivering the last strike.
   - (A) game
   - (B) crowd
   - (C) cheering
   - (D) sportsmanship
   - (E) tension

2. Her_____instincts led her to fund the construction of a hospital for the poor.
   - (A) far-ranging
   - (B) humanitarian
   - (C) humble
   - (D) popular
   - (E) eclectic

3. After years of_____war, the Great Wall was constructed to_____the Chinese people.
   - (A) internecine. . .instigate
   - (B) destructive. . .resurrect
   - (C) unceasing. . .protect
   - (D) amicable. . .unite
   - (E) pitiable. . .win

4. His remarks were so_____that we could not decide which of the possible meanings was correct.
   - (A) facetious
   - (B) ambiguous
   - (C) cogent
   - (D) impalpable
   - (E) congruent

5. FEEL : TOUCH ::
   - (A) tickle : hurt
   - (B) see : look
   - (C) sprint : lift
   - (D) giggle : laugh
   - (E) shed : grow

6. CIRCLE : SQUARE ::
   - (A) ball : bat
   - (B) oval : rectangle
   - (C) sphere : globe
   - (D) angular : straight
   - (E) volume : area

7. CHICKEN : ROOSTER ::
   - (A) deer : doe
   - (B) duck : drake
   - (C) flock : hen
   - (D) ewe : ram
   - (E) pig : piglet

8. TRIGGER : PISTOL ::
   - (A) bullet : gun
   - (B) rifle : revolver
   - (C) guard : police
   - (D) switch : motor
   - (E) fire : shoot

Questions 9–11 are based on the following passage.

Louisa May Alcott (1832–1888) was a beloved author of books for children, but she also wrote gothic tales and short stories for adults. This excerpt is from "Mrs. Gay's Prescription."

The poor little woman looked as if she needed rest but was not likely to get it; for the room was in a chaotic state, the breakfast table presented the appearance of having been devastated by a swarm of locusts, the baby
(5)   began to fret, little Polly set up her usual whine of "I want sumpin to do," and a pile of work loomed in the corner waiting to be done.

"I don't see how I ever shall get through it all," sighed the despondent matron as she hastily drank a
(10)   last cup of tea, while two great tears rolled down her cheeks, as she looked from one puny child to the other, and felt the weariness of her own tired soul and body more oppressive than ever.

"A good cry" was impending, when there came a
(15)   brisk ring at the door, a step in the hall, and a large, rosy woman came bustling in, saying in a cheery voice as she set a flower-pot down upon the table, "Good morning! Nice day, isn't it? Came in early on business and brought you one of my Lady Washingtons, you are
(20)   so fond of flowers."

"Oh, it's lovely! How kind you are. Do sit down if you can find a chair; we are all behind hand today, for I was up half the night with the poor baby, and haven't energy enough to go to work yet," answered Mrs. Bennet,
(25)   with a sudden smile that changed her whole face, while baby stopped fretting to stare at the rosy clusters, and Polly found employment in exploring the pocket of the new comer, as if she knew her way there.

(30)

"Let me put the pot on your stand first, girls are so careless, and I'm proud of this. It will be an ornament to your parlor for a week," and opening a door Mrs. Gay carried the plate to a sunny bay window where many others were blooming beautifully.

(35)

Mrs. Bennet and the children followed to talk and admire, while the servant leisurely cleared the table.

"Now give me that baby, put yourself in the easy chair, and tell me all about your worries," said Mrs. Gay, in the brisk, commanding way which few people could resist.

(40)

"I'm sure I don't know where to begin," sighed Mrs. Bennet, dropping into the comfortable seat while baby changed bearers with great composure.

"I met your husband and he said the doctor had ordered you and these chicks off to Florida for the winter.

(45)

John said he didn't know how he should manage it, but he meant to try."

"Isn't it dreadful? He can't leave his business to go with me, and we shall have to get Aunt Miranda to come and see to him and the boys while I'm gone, and the

(50)

boys can't bear her strict, old-fashioned ways, and I've got to go that long journey all alone and stay among strangers, and these heaps of fall work to do first, and it will cost an immense sum to send us, and I don't know what is to become of me."

(55)

Here Mrs. Bennet stopped for breath, and Mrs. Gay asked briskly, "What is the matter with you and the children?"

"Well, baby is having a hard time with his teeth and is croupy, Polly doesn't get over scarlet fever well,

(60)

and I'm used up; no strength or appetite, pain in my side and low spirits. Entire change of scene, milder climate,

*and less work for me, is what we want, the doctor says.
John is very anxious about us, and I feel regularly
discouraged."*

(65)   *"I'll spend the day and cheer you up a bit. You just
rest and get ready for a new start to-morrow; it is a
saving of time to stop short now and then and see where
to begin next. Bring me the most pressing job of work. I
can sew and see to this little rascal at the same time."*

9. The "little woman" referred to in line 1 is

(A) Lady Washington

(B) Alcott's mother

(C) a servant

(D) Mrs. Bennet

(E) Mrs. Gay

10. When Alcott compares the breakfast table to something "devastated by a swarm of locusts" (line 4), she means

(A) that it is a mess left by an uncaring mob

(B) that children are no more meaningful than insects to Mrs. Bennet

(C) to indicate Mrs. Bennet's flightiness

(D) to illustrate the horror of Mrs. Bennet's life

(E) that the Bennets are pests

11. Had Mrs. Gay not arrived when she did, Alcott leads us to suspect that

(A) Mrs. Bennet would have gone back to bed

(B) the children would have continued to cry

(C) Mrs. Bennet would have accomplished little all day

(D) sickness would have overtaken the entire family

(E) the servant would have left the dishes untended

SECTION 6

8 Questions•Time—10 Minutes

Part 1: Quantitative Comparison Questions

1.

Column A	Column B
$\dfrac{a^2 + b}{2}$	$.5(a^2 + b)$

3. $\dfrac{m}{n} = \dfrac{7}{10}$

Column A	Column B
mn	$90°$

2.

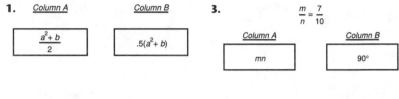

Column A	Column B
x	$90°$

4.   For all real numbers x and y, let $\triangle$ be defined as $x \triangle y = \dfrac{xy}{x - y}$.

Column A	Column B
$-3 \triangle - 2$	$-2 \triangle - 3$

Part 2: Student-Produced Response Questions

5. $(\sqrt{18} - \sqrt{8})^2 =$

6. The distance from the center of a circle to a chord is 5. If the length of the chord is 24, what is the length of the radius of the circle?

7. If the cost of a party is to be split equally among 11 friends, each would pay $15.00. If 20 persons equally split the same cost, how much would each person pay?

8. In the figure below, m∠N=(9x–40)°, m∠J=(4x+30)° and m∠JLR=(8x+40)°. What is the measure of ∠J? (Do not grid the degree symbol.)

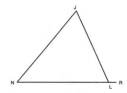

Answer Key

Section 1: Verbal

1. C	6. E
2. E	7. B
3. A	8. D
4. A	9. E
5. C	10. C

Section 2: Math

1. C	5. D
2. C	6. A
3. C	7. D
4. B	8. C

Section 3: Verbal

1. E
2. A
3. D
4. C

Section 4: Math

1. D
2. B
3. B

Section 5: Verbal

1. E	7. B
2. B	8. D
3. C	9. D
4. B	10. A
5. B	11. C
6. B	

Section 6: Math

Part 1	Part 2
1. C	5. 2
2. A	6. 13
3. D	7. 8.25
4. B	8. 70

EXPLANATORY ANSWERS

SECTION 1

1. **(C)** Audience laughter at the wrong moment can easily *disconcert* (upset or confuse) an actor.

2. **(E)** Since the assurances of good faith were *hollow*, it is not surprising that those who made them *reneged* on (went back on) their agreement.

3. **(A)** To win the majority, we must unite, or *amalgamate*, the different factions.

4. **(A)** A primary function of the *throat* is to *swallow*, and a primary function of the *teeth* is to *chew*.

5. **(C)** A *garnet* has the color *red*, and an *emerald* has the color *green*.

6. **(E)** *Patience* is considered one of the *virtues*, just as *literature* is considered one of the *arts*.

7. **(B)** Although Borgia was "reputed cruel," "his cruelty restored Romagna, united it, and brought it to order. . ." (lines 4–5). He used cruelty to good effect, according to Machiavelli.

8. **(D)** In this passage, *signal* means out of the ordinary, or remarkable, as used in "For he who quells disorder by a very few signal examples will be in the end more merciful than he who from too great leniency permits things to take their course and so to result in rapine and bloodshed." One can infer from this that capital punishment as a preventive measure can inhibit capital crimes later, if judiciously applied.

9. **(E)** The idea of balance is present through parallel and contrasting clauses in this paragraph. A Prince should "temper prudence with kindliness" (lines 28–29).

10. **(C)** The last paragraph avers that ". . .it is far safer to be feared than loved. For of men it may be generally affirmed that they are thankless, fickle, false, studious to avoid danger, greedy of gain, devoted to you while you are able to confer benefits upon them, and ready, as I said before, while danger is distant, to shed their blood and sacrifice their property, their lives, and their children for you; but in the hour of need they turn against you."

SECTION 2

1. **(C)** Let the other two angles be $2x$ and $5x$.

   Thus, $2x+5x+82=180$

   $$7x=98$$
   $$x=14$$
   $$2x=28$$
   $$5x=70$$

   Smallest angle $=28°$

2. **(C)** Let $x=$no. of years for 2 populations to be equal.

   Then $6800-120x=4200+80x$

   $$2600=200x$$
   $$x=13$$

3. **(C)** Simply plug the two values into the formula.

   $2^2-2(2)=0$ and $1^2-2(1)=-1$

   $*2-*1=0-(-1)=1$.

4. **(B)**

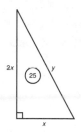

   $\frac{1}{2}\times x\times 2x=25$

   $$x^2=25$$
   $$x=5$$
   $$2x=10$$
   $$y^2=5^2+10^2$$
   $$y^2=25+100$$
   $$y^2=125$$
   $$y=\sqrt{125}=\sqrt{25\times 5}$$
   $$y=5\sqrt{5}$$

5. **(D)** The abscissa of Q is 3 more than that of P. The ordinate of Q is 2 less than that of P. Hence, coordinates of Q are $(3+3, 7-2)=(6,5)$

6. **(A)** $r=5x$

   Divide both sides by 10

   $$\tfrac{r}{10}=\tfrac{5}{10}x$$

   or $\tfrac{1}{10}r=\tfrac{1}{2}x$

   Hence, 1 is the answer.

7. **(D)** The area of triangle ADE equals the area of triangle AEC, since they have the same base and altitude. The area of triangle ABC equals that of triangle ADC, since the diagonal of a parallelogram divides it equally.

8. **(C)** If the side of a square is s, its diagonal is the hypotenuse of a right triangle with two sides as its legs. The length of the diagonal is $\sqrt{s^2+s^2}=\sqrt{2}s$ $0.7(\sqrt{2}s)\approx(0.7)(1.4)s\approx1s=s$.

SECTION 3

1. **(E)** Try out other choices in the context of the sentence, and you will see that only one choice works.

2. **(A)** This is the main idea of paragraph 2, and the author goes so far in lines 16–17 to say that these straight avenues "must give actual pain to a person of taste."

3. **(D)** The root *serpent* helps, but the context of the sentence helps more.

The author is contrasting forced canals and waterfalls to the more natural, winding motion of streams.

4. **(C)** Only Shenstone says (A), and neither author says (B). Both, however, want water to wind naturally instead of appearing forced.

SECTION 4

1. **(D)** $\frac{4}{5}=.8$

$$\frac{7}{9} = 9\overline{)7.00} = .78$$

$$\frac{5}{7} = 7\overline{)5.00} = .71$$

$$\frac{9}{11} = 11\overline{)9.00} = .82$$

Thus, $\frac{5}{7}$ is the smallest quantity.

2. **(B)** Let x=the amount earned each month. $2x$=the amount earned in December.

Then $11x+2x=13x$ (entire earnings).

$$\frac{2x}{13x} = \frac{2}{13}$$

3. **(B)** $3x^3+2x^2+x+1$
$=3(-1)^3+2(-1)^2+(-1)+1$
$=3(-1)+2(1)-1+1$
$=-3+2+0$
$=-1$

4. **(E)** Convert the percent to decimal form before multiplying.
$.03\%=.0003$
$.0003\times.21=.000063$
The number of decimal places in the product must be equal to the sum of the number of decimal places in the terms to be multiplied.

SECTION 5

1. **(E)** *Tension* is likely to mount before a pitcher delivers the last strike of a game—especially during a pause.

2. **(B)** Funding a hospital for the poor may be properly called a *humanitarian* act. It may or may not be popular.

3. **(C)** This is the only answer in which both words are correct in relation to each other as well as to the sense of the sentence.

4. **(B)** The word that means "having more than one meaning" is *ambiguous*.

5. **(B)** When you *touch* something, you *feel* it. Similarly, when you *look* at something, you *see* it.

6. **(B)** The contrast in shape between a *circle* and a *square* is not unlike that between an *oval* and a *rectangle*.

7. **(B)** The male *chicken* is a *rooster*, and the male *duck* is a *drake*.

8. **(D)** A *trigger* activates a *pistol*, and a *switch* a *motor*.

9. **(D)** Introduced as the "little woman" and "despondent matron," Mrs. Bennet is named in paragraph 4. Alcott's epithets for Mrs. Bennet emphasize her weakness.

10. **(A)** Mrs. Bennet's family has left her this mess with as little concern as a swarm of insects might have. Locusts are not particularly horrible; had Alcott used a more potent simile, (D) might be correct.

11. **(C)** Before Mrs. Gay's arrival, Mrs. Bennet was about to have "a good cry" (line 14). There is no indication that she would have been able to cope with her household duties.

SECTION 6

PART 1

1. **(C)** Since dividing by 2 and multiplying by .5 have the same results, the quantities must be equal.

2. **(A)** Since the figure has 5 sides, it contains

    $180(5-2)=540$ degrees

    $540=x+110+60+120+100$

    $540=x+390$

    $150=x$

3. **(D)** The problem tells us only that the ratio of m to n is 7 to 10. It is possible, for example, that m is 700 and n is 1000.

4. **(B)** Simply plug the values into the formula.

   Column A= $\frac{(-3)(-2)}{-3-(-2)} = \frac{6}{-1} = -6$

   Column B= $\frac{(-2)(-3)}{-2-(-3)} = \frac{6}{1} = 6$

Part 2

5. $(\sqrt{18}-\sqrt{8})^2$
   $=(3\sqrt{2}-2\sqrt{2})^2$
   $=(\sqrt{2})^2=2$

6.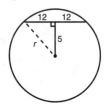

   A radius drawn perpendicular to a chord bisects the chord. Construct the radius as shown above.

   $5^2+12^2=r^2$
   $25+144=r^2$
   $r^2=169$
   $r=13$

7. $\frac{x}{11}=15$
   $x=165$
   $\frac{165}{20}=8.25$

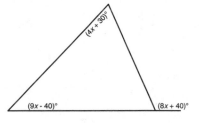

8. An exterior angle of a triangle is equal to the sum of the two remote interior angles.
   $8x+40=(9x-40)+(4x+30)$
   $8x+40=13x-10$
   $5x=50$
   $x=10$
   $m\angle J=(4x+30)°=(40+30)°=70°$

INDEX